BOUNDARY WATERS
CANOE AREA WILDERNESS

Kate Crowley and Mike Link

Photography by

Daniel J. Cox   Sharon Eaton   Michael Furtman
Peter Hawkins   Steve Kuchera   Ron Miles   Ronald Morreim
Peter Roberts   Phil and Judy Sublett

VOYAGEUR PRESS

To Matt, Julie, Alyssa, and Jon,
and their generation,
with the hope that they will leave a legacy of wilderness for their children too

Published by Voyageur Press Inc.
123 North Second Street
Stillwater, Minnesota 55082

ISBN 0-89658-071-7

5   4   3   2   1

Book design by Dimond Graphics
Printed in Singapore by Singapore National Printers Ltd
through Four Colour Imports, Ltd., Louisville KY

CONTENTS

INTRODUCTION

For years I debated doing a book on the Boundary Waters Canoe Area Wilderness (BWCAW). Everyone who uses it knows that it gets too much use. We love it beyond its capacity, and still the United States Forest Service keeps looking for new campsites. I worried that a book on the Boundary Waters would attract too many new people and add to the problem. But Kate and I looked at the current people problems and felt that one of the problems was not the promotion of the land—too many places are promoting it for this book to be a factor in its popularity—but rather one of getting users to understand the country and the fragile heart that lies below its rugged exterior.

It is our hope that this book will add to the literature of Sigurd Olson and others who have touched on the significance of the land, and we hope that we might share our understanding of the ecology in a way that will shape the ethics of the user.

We tell people not to use soap, even biodegradable kinds, in the water, but no one will stop if he or she doesn't care about the life and the beauty. We tell people not to leave fire scars and to keep campsites clean, but that involves effort, and we only make effort when we are forced to or if we care.

Quiet contemplation is something we cherish and request, but it is an act that necessitates a state of mind that goes beyond escaping the city, beyond the wilderness or religious retreat. It is philosophical and ethical, it is personal and fulfilling, but it is not something that people regularly engage in.

For that reason, we have made our book personal. We have taken you to the canoe country through our memories and our thoughts, and we have asked you to look through the eyes of two naturalists who love not only the land but the complexity of the life that lives on it.

When you see us on the waters, don't yell hello across the lake. Paddle over and we'll speak quietly; then we'll know that you too realize our place in canoe country.

(M. Furtman)

Moon Lake (S. Kuchera)

REFLECTIONS

BY MIKE LINK

What greater freedom is there than sitting on a lake with numerous unnamed, unmarked portages to tempt your sense of exploration and discovery? What is more satisfying than the easy movement of a boat over clear, cold waters, propelled by your own energy and sense of time? Where is the wilderness more evident than in a land of ancient rocks, deep lakes, boreal forests, lumbering moose, and the echoing calls of wolves and loons?

The BWCAW is a maze of lakes, portages, hiking trails, bogs, rock ridges, and forests. It is a complex of dreams, visions, history, ecology, and dispute. Men and women have touched this land and felt it in their souls. Writer-philosophers like Sigurd Olson, Aldo Leopold, and Bob Marshall were inspired here.

It has spawned creative works by Helen Hoover, Florence and Lee Jacques, and Calvin Rustrum. It has taken people from their normal paths and required their devotion and dedication to preserve the landscape, the forest, and the solitude. Today we paddle with the spirits of kindred souls, we walk where moccasins and tennis shoes have tread in respect, adventure, and challenge.

Navigate with Fisher maps that mark out portages and campsites and marvel at the pioneer guides and paddlers who had only hand-drawn maps, memory, and a sense of place to guide them from one location to another. Retrace the strokes of history and hear the silent cadence of the voyageur. We raise our paddles to history and to the future, challenged by the fact that this land will always need champions, will always require the voice of the dedicated if it is to remain pristine and inspirational.

The BWCAW is a church, a sanctuary for peace, solitude, and timelessness. It is a place of perspective, a part of the Canadian Shield, a place of three-billion-year-old rocks that have been sculpted by glaciers. Humility is easy when the rock you sit on predates all forms of life.

The mind is soothed with greens and blues and startled by the bright orange lichens on dark rock cliffs. We feel alone in time when the dusk settles in, the sky and the waters meld, the forests are skyline silhouettes and black open spaces, and the thrushes pipe their flutelike notes from the darkness.

We can watch the reflection of sunset hues and drift in liquid clouds that shudder in our passing wake. We drift in our own silence, our minds soothed into a meditative blankness or pouring out the pressures of other days and times that stress our lives. We move in a world of our own, until a pictograph on some lichen-stained rock glows from the past and tells of moose, pelicans, fishing—and Indians.

Then we know why our thoughts are so deep, why our feelings are so rich. Because another person, centuries before, also passed this way, perhaps on an evening like this one, and was so moved by the same kind of beauty and solitude that the rocks became a shrine to thoughts and feelings that could only be expressed in the pictorial language of the day, thoughts that were too important to be lost to time.

We touch kindred souls. We find life reduced to simplicity in this watery world. We drink from the lakes, eat their fish, warm up at fires of downed wood, taste blueberries, admire orchids, swat blackflies and mosquitoes, and envision the ruffed grouse drumming in the distance, its sound so low that we feel it rather than hear it.

We paddle the moonless night across a watery heaven of reflected stars and slide between constellations like a spaceship. Our remembrances of the day are a collection of subtleties, of rock reflections, of dark spruce and light tamarack, of light-barked aspen and birch in a deep green mural.

Mushrooms and mosses, flowers and trees, misshapen trunks, osprey, and eagles all fit together in a matrix of small variations. Beauty is easy to behold here. It is not startling but soothing. It is a juxtaposi-

tion of small changes on a great canvas, and we are not awed by a single dramatic peak but taken into a warm bosom scented by pines.

This is a beauty we cannot capture in a single photograph. There is no one falls, rapids, lake, or tree that typifies the canoe country. There is no one route to take, no single place to visit. It is not a place to be checked off on a list of parks we have seen.

It is to be felt rather than seen. The land is a combination of all the spirits of all who have paddled, hiked, and explored. It is a place that comforts as we seek our own identities.

We can drift in a blackness that lights up under star shine, when both moon and sun are absent. When it is clear, the sky holds stars without number, and the abundance is doubled in reflection. All reflections are doubled and deepened here, so we return again and again to the Boundary Waters for its healing and its inspiration. We experience freedom, and we become renewed. That is the essence of the canoe country; that is the joy of paddling.

(P. Hawkins)

(R. Miles)

Overleaf: Moon Lake (S. Kuchera)

CANOES

BY MIKE LINK

There are boaters of all types in the world. Each person who has taken control of a craft on water has experienced a relationship that goes beyond the human and inanimate. Each boater knows his or her craft by its gender, idiosyncrasies, and beauty. Each has an affair of the heart and mind that nonboaters can only shake their heads at. But the canoeist may have the most intense of all boating relationships.

How do you tell the noncanoeist that this fourteen-to eighteen-foot vessel will be your toy, your moving van, and your constant companion for hours and days; that you will love the experience in the rain, when there is no roof to keep you dry and the boat bottom creates a private wading pool. We have affection for this craft that won't go straight with regular strokes, that wants to turn broadside in large waves, and drifts in the wind. This boat is special to us, even though we supply the power on the water and carry it on our backs on land.

It is one of the rare sensations of life, when canoe and canoeist become one. We depend on the boat, but the boat is helpless without us and requires our energy. We sit or kneel, and we drive our strength through the paddles into the water. We extend our spirit as well as our muscles, and the boat responds.

As we develop skills, learn the little twists of the blade, the angles of stroke, the responses of the hull, and the variations in wave, weather, and packing, we become more of an extension of the boat. The hull responds to shifts of weight, our arms extend in natural rhythms of movement, the water swirls off the blades, the boat leaves a small straight wake in its path, and shorelines both disappear and grow.

It is a sense of accomplishment that fuels our spirit. It is a sense of adventure that gives us inspiration and renews our energy. We enjoy the canoe because it is more than us. We earn our distance; we find our point of beauty. We take the world on its own terms. We pull into a rocky campsite, unload our gear, and eat a fire-cooked meal with a greater relish, with a primitive satisfaction.

Beauty that we earn by physical and mental effort, by leaving the human trail, seems more lasting, more spiritual than that which we drive to, climb steps for, and hold onto rails to see. Beauty in the canoe is a constant companion. We are immersed in it and constantly absorb the greens and blues, the reflections and variations.

The trip is marked by rock exposures and unusual tree shapes. Everything passes slowly. It begins as a blue-green blur that intensifies in color, enriches with details, and slides gracefully into the distance again. While the body and the canoe move together, the eyes can probe the chorus of the forest and the mind can run the gamut of personal reflection.

There are moments when the present blurs, the Indians and voyageurs emerge, and we are in a stream of history with birchbark companions. We sense both place and time, and our craft, no matter what the design, is part of this grand lineage. It is a time machine.

When we finally leave the water, the boat comes with us, riding with keel to the wind on top of our vehicle. It comes laden with memories, and when we sand the hull, spread the epoxy, varnish the gunwales, recane the seats, or sit and stare at it when the temperature is forty below, memories will flow back with the breeze and sun of summer to lift us back in time once more.

That is the magic of the canoe. We will also turn our heads when another vehicle passes us with a canoe on top. We will smile at the novice's zigzag route and remember our own beginnings. We will pause as we drive over bridges and pass by lakeshores.

There will always be another corner to turn, another lake to drift. We will forget the hard days, the wet and cold times, and focus on the spiritual renewal that our canoe provided. We will seek the next portage, dream over maps, listen for lakes with exotic Indian names, and kneel on our living room floor with water and sun in our hearts. That is the beauty of canoeing. It never ends.

Kawishiwi River (D. Cox)

Overleaf : Lake Polly on the Sawbill Trail (S. Kuchera)

(R. Miles)

MAPS, MEMORIES AND DREAMS

BY MIKE LINK

Spread before me is a piece of imagination. Some would call it a map, but to me it is a dream fabric woven with lines that are tied to the soul. In the length of a winter's night, with wood burning in the stove, the glow of the lamp reflecting on the window frost, and the hint of a wind humming in the darkness, my Superior National Forest map spreads out on the living room floor, transporting me to cool streams under a hot sun, to quiet campsites, and to rock ledges where daydreams take birth.

I can spread the Fisher maps and see their contours rise in three-dimensional landscapes. The red swathes become leafy portages, and the red dots are invitations to pitch a tent, build a fire, and string a hammock. Everywhere the call is to explore and to be immersed. All the campsites are pristine in my winter dreams, and all the lakes are empty of other humans.

As I slip into a map world, I find my mind playing various games with the lakes. Each name is a notation in history. Each name connotes some inspiration, some fleeting impression. They are fun for the moments of thoughtfulness that they inspire.

There is Crocodile Lake in the midst of this boreal wonderland, and it sits right below a much more appropriate wildlife name—Bearskin. Was there a bearskin there? Did some Indian leave it behind? Is it even important to know the truth? It is also south of Flour Lake. Did the camp cook name this? Or did the bag of flour fall out of the canoe? Indian names like Watap, Kiskadinna, Gijikiki, and Makwa seem appropriate. There is a certain romantic feeling that we associate with these names. Perhaps it is our own romanticized feeling that only the Indian saw this land as true wilderness.

In contrast to these rolling syllables, we find the imaginative quartet of Lakes One, Two, Three, and Four. Maybe it was just a bad day for the cartographer who had to fill the map with the one thousand different lake names. In frustration, he threw up his arms and announced, "Alright we'll just call them Wednesday, Thursday, Friday, and Saturday bays." He is probably related to the person who named This Man, That Man, No Man, and Other Man lakes.

There are many human names. We have Homer, Otto, Winchell, Gordon, Davis, Dawkins, Carol, Alice, Ada, Phoebe, and Polly. We don't know who these people were, but don't you wonder how they rated such a distinctive and lasting monument?

Some of the names are fun to say, syllables that tickle the tongue like Ogishkemuncie, Kekekabic, Banadad, and Kawishiwi. But to bring balance, there are some like Ge-be-on-e-quet.

Perhaps more appropriately than Homo sapiens, other animals have also made their way into the lake lexicon. There is Loon, Caribou, Duck, Moose, Oyster, Pike, and Honker. Were they named because the animals were observed there? Or were they just more fillers on the blue blanks of some office map?

There are some stories out there too: What was the Disappointment? What fell in Splash Lake? Was it lunchtime when Pickle, Bean, Tomato, Onion, and Cucumber were named? Or had a seed catalog just arrived? Is the sequence of Smoke, Flame, and Burnt lakes a descriptive story in and of itself? Doesn't Greenwood River's original name, Diarrhoea, create a more interesting story?

I can travel these routes in the canoe of my mind and return to old routes and lakes and portages. Memories wait there, images of past satisfactions and beauty.

THE ARROWHEAD TRAIL

BY MIKE LINK

The Arrowhead Trail is one of the least known of the roads that leads to the lakes of the BWCAW. It begins at Hovland, where Chicago Bay forms a cove in Lake Superior's volcanic shoreline, and parallels the Flute Reed River as it begins to wind north. The road crosses more state and Indian land than national forest, and water is scarcer here than on any other canoe country access road. Small streams like Swamp River and Irish Creek cross the road, but very few lakes can be seen in the forest. The trail terminates at McFarland Lake, close to the Canadian border.

Along the Arrowhead Trail, the relief is dramatic and the fall coloration is more varied than in most locations. There are narrow dirt roads that wander from the main gravel road, but they are few and far between and lack the names and feeling that would invite you to digress from your route.

Access to the beautiful Border Lakes Trail beginning is found near Otter Lake. It is an area of large, linear lakes along the country's border and large north-facing cliff faces.

This is the country of the Logan Intrusions, a sandwich landscape where volcanic rocks squeezed between the layers of softer sedimentary rocks. It is a place where the flat layers were tilted in one of the earth's massive shrugs. The rocks jut up, layer after layer, broken and jagged. The hard layers resisted the glacier, and the glacial ice and streams cut away at the soft layers and left the harder rocks as cliff faces. Frost took over when the glacier was gone, and sequences of freezing, thawing, and refreezing slowly reshaped the cliff faces, sending frost-wedged boulders to rest in the talus slopes beneath the escarpments.

The drama of the land reaches right out of McFarland Lake and invites the canoeist into the water. It feels mountainous here. Canoes seem dwarfed. In the fall, the slopes that rise from the water are color mosaics, and the morning mists lift like clouds in the mountains from perched lake basins that are hidden in the forest.

Johnson Falls at the west end of Pine Lake is a mist-shrouded canyon that is filled with one of the canoe country's most spectacular cataracts. It is a small stream that plunges and twists over a narrow rock bed. The grades are steep and wet, the light is seldom ever good for photography, but the falls is a perfect place to lose yourself in the soothing roar of water that deletes all other sound from experience.

It was a beautiful, sunny autumn day when I first went to the falls and decided that I would go overland with my group rather than follow the stream. We went to the ridge top and enjoyed the sunlight filtering through the canopy. It was warm, and soft light blanketed the lichen-covered rock.

We walked for awhile in the direction opposite the falls and were rewarded with the sight of a ruffed grouse that was resting within a large moose track. As we approached quietly, the bird rose from the track and walked into the undergrowth. It was a fitting climax for that walk, so we decided to return to the portage trail and head to the falls.

Three of our group, Ginny, Larry, and John, had already turned back. But when we got to the trail, they weren't there. I walked to the end of the portage, and they weren't there either. We checked the opposite end, but there was no sign of them on that end either. We couldn't imagine them just going on without us, but tracks indicated that they weren't behind us. Although they had succeeded in returning to the portage, it seemed they had just kept walking.

We fanned out and set up a search pattern. "Larry, Ginny, John!" No response. We moved our sweep teams in, paused, called, but got no response. We maintained our group communications and for the next hour moved slowly west, listening, calling, watching. Then at one pause I heard, "Yoohoo!" I called, but John and Larry are hard of hearing and Ginny was giving such a steady barrage of *yoohoo*s that she forgot to listen for a response. We were reunited, and all of our spirits were raised.

Bald eagle (P. Roberts)

Canoeists paddle through a river of wild rice. (D. Cox)

(R. Morreim)

Two of us were exploring the Royal River and entered its massive rice and rush beds to find a large flock of migrating waterfowl. We were ecstatic as the birds took wing all around us and flew off over the trees. Then we heard the flurry of guns that greeted them on South Fowl. We turned around and left. It wasn't the same undisturbed wilderness that we had come to find. Solitude is a bargain between all the inhabitants, and we were not ready for this.

A bald eagle has greeted each of my paddles past the islands of West Pike Lake. The eagle would sit in the tall pines on the island, and each time I canoed past this large, white-headed bird, I was impressed with its size and majestic image.

On Mountain Lake, it is the cliff that creates the feeling of mountains. The rock face rising from the water to tower hundreds of feet above gives the canoeist a sense of humility. The sense of harmony with nature is often a product of relativity. We need the perspective of our own importance and position in the scheme of nature, and a rock mass has a cold ability to let us know how small we really are in size and lifespan.

Johnson Falls (S. Kuchera)

THE GUNFLINT TRAIL

BY MIKE LINK

The road north from Grand Marais is longer and much more complex than the Arrowhead. It is also much more used. This road is paved, and climbs from the harbor over the crest of the Superior highlands. The highlands are part of a volcanic rock episode that dates back to the creation of Lake Superior. In the fall, the maples that line the ridges give the canoe country streaks of orange and red.

The Gunflint Trail has numerous resorts, and many roads branch off along the way. There are tempting side trips, campgrounds, and cabins that invite the explorer, and lakes peek from the woods with promises of a moose in their remoteness. The driver should be alert to wildlife along the trail. Moose emerge suddenly to cross the road in front of cars, and bears saunter along the gravel. Grouse sometimes pick up gravel from the shoulders, and small mammals will cross the road for a change of scenery.

There are many entry points from the Gunflint. Some are remote and must be discovered by personal effort. These are the special places that the "regulars" know, the ones that aren't so obvious on a map. They usually require more physical effort. There are also many places that are accessible and obvious but still offer the canoeist a special experience.

I took a solo paddle on the Granite River one late September. The river has some small navigable rapids and some areas where a portage is the only acceptable route. There are great granite domes that form islands in the larger portions on the river, bare rock with only a few hardy trees and pioneering plants.

The trip began on a sunny day. Most people assume that the entire route is the Granite, but the river begins at Granite Lake. The entry is the Pine River, which passes between rocks of the Gunflint Iron Formation.

I played with my compass near the rock. It was moved by the bedrock, and I was satisfied. I paddled on and slowly explored the waterway, lounged on the rocks near the falls, laid in the sun, wrote in my journal, and listened to the flocks of crossbills in the treetops.

Every portage is a trail to new adventure.

(D. Cox)

In the shadows of the dark rocks that line the waterway are rafts of water smartweed, with their delicate mix of pinks and whites and their floating green leaves. On the dark waters, they seemed to possess an internal light.

It was an interesting trip for other reasons as well. I had divided my food with two other people, and I hadn't been too picky in doing the dividing. This meant I had no seasonings and almost no variety. On the third day out, I began to crave a drink with some flavor. Even canoe country water loses its excitement when that is all that you have to drink. The day was grey, oppressively grey, and even the sweep of water between giant granite arms wasn't brightening it.

I met a couple that afternoon, setting up a new camp. Most of the time I stay away from others because I expect that many of them are like me and want to have maximum solitude, but this time I could not resist. They had one envelope of cocoa that they could spare, and I paddled on planning how I would stretch the envelope that evening. I conversed with a red squirrel at that night's campsite and enjoyed two thin cups of the best cocoa I had ever tasted.

Continuing my journey, the first notice that I was approaching Saganaga Lake was a swatch of burnt-over area that came from Sag to my route. Sag has experienced many fires over the years. Its arms and bays are a variety of ages, all relating to the various fires and the fickle paths that the flames chose to follow.

In the midst of every burn, there are trees that were missed for reasons too complex for casual explanation. They were in positions where wind eddies took the flames in different routes. They were protected by rocks, or the branches were above the fire level and the bark withstood the heat.

There are rows and clumps of pines and aspens, a fine sea of green and gold in the fall, where the fire damage is most extensive. Here the trees show their adaptation to fire and demonstrate how natural fire is as an agent of ecological diversity. The jack pine cones are serotinous, which means that they are glued together by their own resin and require fire to melt the resin, release the scales, and let the seeds disperse. The pines tend to be in thick clumps that smother competitors. The aspen have a different tactic. They may sprout from seeds but are more likely to rise as sprouts from the roots of past aspens and take to the new sun-lit forest floor. They grow rapidly, attaining heights that will help them to compete with the shading conifers.

On the ground, there are new pioneer plants, plants that need full sunshine and new mineral soils. Here the blackened soil absorbs the sun's energy, heats the new seed, and coaxes life from it. There are fireweeds soon after a burn and lesser known green plants that help to reestablish the plant community.

The blackened trunks are rich with insects to aid in decomposition and woodpeckers anxious to control the insect population. Deer and moose gather the soil in their mouths and enjoy the rich mineral salts. They will return later to consume the new young shoots as they appear above the snow, just as the mice enjoy the fresh sprouts and the succulent cambium on new growth. Blueberries and cherries come in soon after a fire, and their rich fruits attract more birds and browsing bear. As we look closer at its complexity, the fire area becomes a rich piece of the forest mosaic and loses the feeling of disaster.

Having paddled past this burnt-over area, I look at the surrounding forest and see it as a patchwork of different ages. There are tracks of past fingers of flame as they swept through the various rock ridges and valleys in long-forgotten fires.

Hiking to Roy Lake from a bay of Saganaga Lake, I walked the old portage trail across wet firefalls and stepped through thick post-fire brush. In 1976, the Boundary Waters had experienced severe drought conditions throughout the summer. It was so dry that the forest service first outlawed fires, then followed with a ban on travel due to the danger. It was a year of difficult work for the forest service fire crews.

At Roy Lake, a fire began that year on August 21. The summer had been one of the driest on record, and only .58 inches of rainfall had been recorded for the normally wet period of April 26 through June 6. The canoe country then experienced a series of thunderstorms in which there was a significant amount of lightning but low amounts of rain, and in July the drought resumed. On the morning of August 21, thunderstorms appeared, and light sprinkles accompanied the lightning. Because the morning had high humidity, a fire that had been started by lightning smouldered until the humidity lowered and the sky cleared in midmorning. By then, the fire was well developed, and the blaze took off through the dry forest.

The fire rode the ridges and leaped some valleys. In other places, it took the valley route and swept downward in an all-consuming blaze. The fire was finally contained at the Seagull River.

After the fire, the forest was blackened with pockets of spruce and hardwoods intermittently scattered among the granite ridges. The rocks were a startling pink because the lichens and mosses had been burnt off, and the granite contrasted with the blackness. It was a stark landscape, but more significant was that by October, a smattering of green plants had been added to the forest. Life had not waited for a new season; it had not delayed for planting. Already flowers and spreading rhizomes were obvious. It was a terrific example of ecological strength.

Now I was back after eight years, and the landscape was a carpet of green jack pine and golden aspen, rivers of color and life flowing from Roy Lake through the hills and off to other lakes and streams. It represented ribbons of life and variations of age, new additions to the mosaic of communities that we value as the scenery of canoe country.

I found strong evidence of recent moose activity at Roy Lake, and the entire area delighted me. Then, as so often happens in the wilderness, the unplanned event took place. I turned to go back to my canoe and stepped on a blackened tree that had not yet decomposed—part of the tangle from the burning, the wind, the subsequent foraging and rotting. It was wet from the rain of the previous two days, and it was slippery. My foot came down on the wood and slipped off, twisting my ankle.

I felt the sudden twinge of excited nerve receptors reacting to the stretch and twist of ligaments. I winced as it happened, and my body felt a jolt and shock that moved to my lower back. There was a pain in the lower back, a stronger pain, that made the ankle a forgettable part of my body. I bent over sharply and felt the soreness radiate with every movement. My steps became gingerly and hesitant. A branch served as a staff and a balance as well as a support.

The trip to the canoe was anguishingly slow. I stepped and fell into the boat, adjusted my posture so that I could paddle with the least amount of torque, and paddled out. The islands of the red rock bay were beautiful, and the burnt-over area was interspersed with mature forest stands, but the beauty wasn't registering as I would have liked. At the portage, I lay on the ground, listened to two merlins call from a white pine, and tried to determine a strategy for getting across to Red Rock Lake and then to Alpine.

It was a matter of bracing myself with a canoe paddle under an armpit, a staff in one hand, and a pack and a canoe balanced on my back. I didn't want to twist, because that intensified the pain. The portages grew in my consciousness. Once I got to Alpine Lake, I was determined to get onto Seagull, because that was where I would meet my students and staff.

I looked at the portage and the river it tried to avoid and decided I didn't want to try another carry. I didn't think that I could make it. Whatever the river had, seemed better. Here the river had small rapids rather than the big drop, and it had the rains of a wet year to make it canoeable. I was determined not to make a mistake. Each small rapids was a challenge to run clean with minimum effort. I slid out of the river ex-

hausted and entered Seagull Lake in the last light of the day.

I found an island campsite, pulled up to it, and had to roll out of the boat onto the rock. The muscles in my back were now cramping severely, and the night cold and dampness were making it impossible to loosen up. I dragged my boat onto the rock and crawled with my pack to a tent site.

There would be no campfire tonight, no cooked supper, no bear bag in the tree. It was a warm, dry sleeping bag I craved and some aspirin. Inside my bag, I downed the aspirin, but my relief was only a partial one. What I had in my first-aid kit was not pure aspirin but Anacin, which includes caffeine in its active ingredients. Each time the muscles relaxed, the caffeine kicked in, and I spent the entire night reading and finishing John McPhee's *Coming Into the Country*.

The next day, tired, my back a little better, sunshine to warm my soul and my body, I paddled out.

Gaskin and Winchell lakes are also lakes of the Gunflint Trail. They are part of other routes and different conditions. They are, in fact, part of the ribbon of lakes that ties the Brule Lake access and the Gunflint area together.

These lakes are linear waterways, old river channels that have been blocked by glacial deposits, part of the streams that cut the Ozark-like terrain before the ice came. High hills rise on the distant horizon — the Misquah Hills, which are the highest points of land in Minnesota. The name Misquah is from the Indians and refers to the reddish color of the rocks that make up most of them.

Gaskin Lake evokes memories of moose wading into the bays and eating the submerged vegetation, and osprey flying around their nest with food for their young. The nest is perched right on top of a dead tree, like most osprey nests. It is a marvelous construction of twigs in a large round cup, and it defies the imagination more than any nest I know of. How do you begin a round nest on top of a pole? How do you begin to weave the sticks into the cup shape? How do you balance the structure? How do you support it without angled posts or guy lines? These nests last not only the nesting season but many seasons.

On Winchell Lake, it is the massive rock cliff on the south shore and the narrow peninsula of a campsite that are most attractive. The cliff is a vertical line of rocks with a far distant view. Here you can watch other canoeists or transform yourself into a windblown spirit that soars about the waters and wildlife. You can play on the rocks, or contemplate, but never should you have to hear unwanted noise. Here your thoughts range over the countryside, and any noise would sweep off the cliff like a harsh stroke of unnatural thunder. Winchell tends to get a lot of traffic, and that can be a real drawback if all the users aren't aware of one another and their collective impact.

Spruce grouse (D. Cox)

25

THE CARIBOU TRAIL

BY MIKE LINK

One of the least-known entry roads to canoe country leaves the lake shore just north of Lutsen. The Caribou Trail is named for an animal that was quite abundant before the influx of European settlers. These woodland caribou differed from the tundra caribou in their behavior and in their habitat, but they still carried the large antlers that make the caribou so unmistakable.

For generations, the caribou moved in the forested areas and ate lichens from the rocks and the tree branches. They browsed on woody plants and fed the timber wolves. They were the upland counterpart to the moose, and for both of these magnificent animals, the land was a harmonious and rich ecological area. Then the loggers came.

To feed the camps, loggers shot the caribou, which proved to be an easy prey. The ax and the fires that followed the cuttings removed the lichens and foods that were natural to the caribou. They lost their shelter and seclusion, and they lost their sustenance. The new growth that followed the loggers was similar to what had always followed the destruction of the forest. But unlike fires and windstorms, loggers cleared massive areas of land, making the successional forest the dominant forest.

Into this new environment came a new addition to the wildlife of the Boundary Waters. Following an abundant food source that was richer than it had encountered in all its years of evolution, the white-tailed deer became the most abundant large ungulate. It also introduced another animal species to the ecological complex, the brain worm, which is lethal to both caribou and moose. By the 1920s the caribou were gone.

Now the forest is returning to its old and natural status. The whitetail is dying off, and the moose is gaining in population. The stage is set for the caribou to return. In the early 1980s, two caribou actually wandered down the North Shore Highway like tourists from Canada. They got as far as Grand Marais, and then no one saw them again.

The land along the Caribou Trail is heavily wooded, and many side roads enter it. In many ways this trail seems like it could be in any of the large northern forests. There are some pretty lakes along the way, but it does not have the distinctive feeling of the canoe country. The lakes are too scattered here, and the side roads seem too civil. But it is a good fall color road, and it is a beautiful wooded trail.

The Caribou Trail ends at another forest road, and there are two distinct choices to make at the intersection. To the right is the trail to Eagle Mountain, and to the left is the road to Brule Lake.

Eagle Mountain is Minnesota's highest point. It is accessible by a footpath that winds past a small lake, through wetlands, across streams, and through forest. The trail is like a transect line, a path that researchers create by compass bearing for sampling an area's vegetation and wildlife in a study area. It is a short walk, and it has all the variety that you could ask for in this region. The last part of the trail winds up the hill, with a few switchbacks. But this is Minnesota, and the elevation does not rob you of breath the way the western peaks do.

On top, there is a panorama of lakes, streams, and forest. It is better than a fire tower, for here you still touch the earth. The forest is not just beneath you, it is all around you. Here solid rock spills over the cliffs and connects you with the landscape that you are viewing. There are clouds that float by, blue skies, and distant, beckoning horizons, but you are part of the land here, part of the richness of the Superior National Forest, and part of the feeling of wilderness. And you have earned that feeling by your own efforts.

If you had gone the other way, to Brule Lake, you would have found a small bay to enter a giant lake. Nestled in these Misquah Hills, Brule Lake has the same qualities of size and breadth that the highlands have. It is a part of a Paul Bunyan landscape. To paddle Brule is to work. There is no easy way to cross this lake. It is always a great distance to the point you want

Fall scene (P. Hawkins)

to gain, and unless you watch your map, the bays and peninsulas will change as you approach them, and portages will hide in thick forests.

When the wind rolls in from the west, it has a long stretch of water to roil up. The waves roll over each other, pushing one another to higher and higher crests until huge rollers stream past the islands and crash on the eastern shore. Navigating this lake in strong winds is a challenge; it is a matter of quartering the waves, paddling up liquid hills, and then not sliding too quickly into the liquid wall ahead of you. It is a challenge to avoid the white froth as it breaks beside your gunwales, threatening to cascade into your canoe.

There is nothing easy about this paddle, no relaxation for the bow or the stern until you get behind an island or a point of land. The waves will await your reemergence, and if you become fatigued or lose your concentration, there is a chilly swim to reawaken you.

Brule isn't always violent. Sometimes it is almost like glass, a mirror with islands that take wing and ride suspended on the horizon as the light waves play in the differing densities of air above the cool water. It

is on these days that the song of the Swainson's thrush reverberates from the tree trunks and the cries of the gulls seem harsh and human.

Bald eagles perch on the lofty southern shoreline trees and watch for feeding opportunities, such as a fish that comes up too close to the surface or an osprey with a fresh catch they can bully away.

In the midst of the lake, there is another attraction, *The Lady of Brule Lake*. On a rock in the middle of the lake is a larger-than-life statue of an Indian woman made of wire mesh and poured concrete. It is a curiosity for the canoeist, a variation on the green hills and the loons. It is symbolic of ventures on the lake, and in a mystical sense, it is a symbol of our dreams and the kinds of objects that are infused in our various religions. Here in the midst of all the natural beauty, we still reach out with our own sense of need and perception. The *Lady of Brule Lake* is for all the dreamers who paddle by, whether they hate her as something out of place, view her with neutral curiosity, or attach to her their own mystical symbolism.

(R. Morreim)

White-tailed deer fawn (P. and J. Sublett)

THE SAWBILL TRAIL

BY MIKE LINK

From the town of Tofte, the Sawbill Trail heads north. Shortly after leaving the shore, Carlton Peak rears up to the south. Although there are taller peaks, Carlton has a shape that is the most distinctive. It has trails on it, and quarrying operations have etched new lines on its profile. It is a climber and hiker's paradise.

Further up the trail, there is a blister-rust research area. The majestic white pines of the state had been threatened by an insidious plague called white pine blister rust, which had a history similar to the Dutch elm disease. Both of these attacks on our native trees originated in our exchange of goods with other continents. They are introduced pathogens, which our native species lack a defense for.

Blister rust has an ecology that requires an intermediary host to enter the cycle. The rust must move from various *Ribes* plants to the white pine. During the Depression, armies of Civilian Conservation Corps workers ravaged the state's forests in an attack on the gooseberry host to control the disease. Fortunately, there are still gooseberries left; even more importantly, we still have the white pine in our forest inventories.

The Sawbill Trail also has a deer/snowshoe-hare/moose exclosure that demonstrates some important ecological factors. An exclosure is designed to eliminate browsers from a limited area of forest.

All of our forest areas begin with many more plants than we have in a mature forest stand. The plants that begin the cycle of succession together compete and eliminate one another through shading, competition for nutrients and water, and physical crowding. But there is another factor in survival. The wildlife of an area, from the mice to the moose, selects what will survive by what they choose not to eat.

In this exclosure, the mice are the only selectors. You can see a marked difference between the exclosed and the available forests.

The Sawbill Trail is a good wildlife road. Lakes are not part of the scenery, but the Temperance River is a constant companion, paralleling the road most of the way and crossing it further north.

The trail is named for the merganser, perhaps the most common type of waterfowl in the canoe country. The merganser is a diving duck, a specialized family that includes the red-breasted, common, and hooded mergansers. They are divers that rival the loon for efficiency underwater, and they can be found on both lakes and streams. Because they are fish eaters, the edges of their bills have serrations that work in place of teeth for grip. It is this toothed bill that gives them the nickname sawbills.

Most of the lakes in this area have low shorelines — no large cliffs or high valleys, just a water's edge forest that leads into deeper woods. On Cherokee Lake, there are many rock ledges and tongues that are inviting to the explorer and the daydreamer. Loons and gulls lay their eggs on Cherokee, and merganser families explore the stream on the southwest corner.

During one trip to The Boundary Waters, I camped at a campsite on the east side of Cherokee Lake that had many tall cedars nearby and tall, spindly pines. I wanted to get my bear rope over one of the high tree limbs, so I tied a piece of wood to the end of the rope to give it weight. I spun the rope to gain momentum and let it sail. It went over the branch I'd aimed for, and I tugged the line to stop the stick's momentum. The line halted instantly, and the reverse momentum caused the wood to sail back under the branch and smack against the trunk of a neighboring pine. As soon as it hit, a flurry of wings came from the trunk itself, emerging from a hole I had not seen. A small saw-whet owl flew to another branch, watched us, dove over my head and onto another branch where it sat, watched our entire operation, and waited until we were done and blackness covered its airborne trail to take its leave.

That night, my companion and I paddled across the lake to visit an island campsite where some of my students were camped. My partner had been my first

Great blue heron (P. Roberts)

A family of common mergansers—mother and young—swim along a shoreline. Their serrated bills have given them the nickname sawbills. (S. Kuchera)

Casting into the sunset on Lake Polly. (D. Cox)

serious canoe partner, the man who shared my canoes on wild races down the Black River in Wisconsin and who had learned to canoe in the same school of trial and error where I had studied. We had capsized together, run waters that we should have portaged, felt the sting of white froth borne on strong head winds, plunged into foamy curls of rapids, and laughed at the exhilarating demands that fast water had made on us. We had felt the energy of running water, and we cherished it. But on this night, leaving my students behind in the blackened night of a moonless sky, we experienced just the opposite of those hair-raising runs.

This night was so calm that our blackened bow wake rolled into the darkness like giant waves, and we could hear them lap on the distant shore. All the shorelines melded into the darkness and were set apart from the sky only because these places lacked stars. The sky was clearer and the stars more brilliant than anyplace I had ever been, even "Big Sky Country." On this night and this paddle, I knew why the stars could have such an impact.

We were not a canoe any longer, we were a spaceship, gliding quietly from constellation to constellation. Our boat was no longer earthbound. We could plot our way between the stars and cross the Milky Way. Our efforts were easy, our strokes were muted in an agreement that was never spoken. The night was magic, and shooting stars passed across our bow. By the time we returned to our camp, we had experienced a whole new feeling of peace and solitude, space and time. For all the wild paddles that we taken, nothing had compared with this moment for its lasting impression.

On a side trip from Cherokee up to Town and Cash lakes, I discovered a heron rookery on a large rock island. They seemed out of place in this loon land. The great blue heron is a common bird on the swamps, marshes, and ponds of the continent. They are awkward-looking birds, throwbacks to the prehistoric swamps, ancient silhouettes flying between cypress and cedar, between the Carboniferous swamps and the Holocene bogs.

Here in rock-dominated boreal country I don't expect to see great blue herons. But although they are less abundant, they are present, searching the shallows of the boreal streams and spearing the small fish and the large frogs. I have watched them move from bend to bend as I floated downstream, seeming to resent my presence but refusing to acknowledge the inevitable drift of the current. They stand frozen, stare, then unleash their massive wings, spring from their long legs, emit a gush of whitewash, and bellow the loud, coarse croak that has echoed through time.

Northeast of Cherokee, the Frost River moves past a sequence of beaver dams and winds along a hard and occasionally too-shallow route. It flows from Frost Lake, which is one of those lakes that just doesn't seem to belong. The shoreline of Frost has crescent beaches of sand—soft, light-colored sand that rivals the beaches of fine resorts, beaches like those around the lake country of central Minnesota, not the rock ledges or steep drops of the canoe country. Here you can walk from the beach in sand that spreads evenly and with little slope. You feel like you can walk across the lake, and perhaps you can if you are persistent. Frost Lake is a glacial lake like all of the rest, but this one marks a place of glacial drainage, a place where running water sorted the rough cobbles and grit of the melting glacier and left the even texture of sand to mark the course of the water's movement. It is one more example of the unexpected, the simple but dramatic variations on a theme of water, woods, and sky that constitute lake country in the North.

(R. Miles)

THE FERNBERG ROAD

BY MIKE LINK

Was this road named for the old city of Fern? The old town was given its name by a vote of the citizens, who represented a wide range of ethnic groups. The road connects the Ely area with Winton (named for the superintendent of the building of the Winton Sawmill in 1898) and the complex of resorts and outfitters on Fall, Moose, Snowbank, Farm, and other large lakes along the road.

The road is a short, dead-end route that terminates at the Kawishiwi River. The route winds over a rolling terrain and features nice views of some small lakes and streams. There are good rock outcrops along the road, part of the Giants Range batholith (a very large granite formation) and the volcanic rocks of the Ely Greenstone. Like the area near the tip of the Gunflint Trail, this part of the canoe country has a complicated combination of intrusive, extrusive, sedimentary (iron formation), and metamorphic rocks.

This area is a window into the Precambrian, one of the classic places on earth to view the longest and most complex period of the earth's development. In most places, the old rocks have been covered by new sediments, and the Precambrian rocks form the basement, the support structure for the newer rock types. They are covered by glacial deposits and hidden where only drilling can bring clues to the surface. Here the glacier did not completely cover the rocks with its meltwater detritus, but instead it scoured away other materials and left intriguing rock faces for lichens and geologists.

Geologists from Winchell, for whom the lake is named, to John Green of the University of Minnesota at Duluth have explored this vast area for the rock stories in the mines, the road cuts, the cliffs, and the stream valleys. They have found gold, copper, nickel, and other precious metals. They have located lava flows that solidified in pillow shapes because they cooled underwater, and they have seen relationships between stratas, complex swirling bands of iron, volcanic bombs that cooled in the air and dropped back

into still liquid flows. There are stories here that relate to the very beginning of our continent and to the development and evolution of the planet.

Stopping by some rock flows, we can look back over three billion years. It is the type of experience that we can feel but never truly understand. Geologic time and human time function on such different scales that we are not truly comprehending, but we can be thrilled by the effort.

Geologist and ecologist Sigurd Olson came to this area and found his dreams fulfilled. He worked the area lakes as a guide and had a partnership in an outfitting firm in Winton. At that time, visitors came to the area by train, and the last stop was at Winton. Sig would greet his new customers at the train, take them to the store, outfit them, and head out of Fall Lake. They would then pursue the fish and scenery of their dreams.

Now the Fernberg Trail and the region have changed. The roads that we take into the canoe country are valued excursions into a beautiful area. We can enjoy the views and the accesses that the roads provide. But all of us who have used this area with frequency and have developed a love for the lake lands realize how small this thousand-lake complex really is, and we know how damaging it would be to have any more roads and any more accesses built here.

With all the smaller entry points that are not included in this book, it is almost impossible to get to lakes that require more than two days' paddling from a put-in spot. When you paddle further than two days, you are seldom rewarded with the extra solitude that you feel you have earned. Instead, you begin to meet travelers from other routes seeking the same privacy that you crave.

Roads are for resorts, for motors, for people who don't want to experience the backcountry but want a glimpse of the countryside. To a limited extent, they satisfy the urge we all have to at least touch the countryside and to experience it a little if time does not allow us the chance to fulfill our needs completely. These are avenues for the wilderness voyeur who can only wish for the opportunity to be a voyageur.

The Fernberg and some other roads in the canoe country were pirated into the landscape. They were bulldozed while our country concentrated on war, and they were done for profiteering individuals who saw dollar signs instead of the grandiose beauty of the whole. They would have chopped up and divided the countryside into a checkerboard if there had not been people to champion the cause of the wilderness.

My first canoe trip in this area began on Moose Lake. It was a beautiful May day, and my companions on the trip were other members of the now-defunct Department of Natural Resources advisory board. We were going to spend three days on Ensign Lake to discuss the problems of canoe country as they related to the state. What I learned was a great respect for this land, a love of its open horizons, a craving for its solitude.

I will always remember the echoing calls of the chipmunks and the taste of walleyes grilled on the fire. I still think of the woodland jumping mouse that provided so much entertainment at the throne it was difficult to remember why I had walked back into the woods in the first place. The memory of my first skinny-dip off a secluded rock ledge and the satisfaction of slipping quietly into a sheltered bay is accompanied by the call of a circling broad-winged hawk and the sight of a bald eagle crossing the bay.

My strongest memory of this trip is of a walk with a man named Richard C. Davids, an author and magazine editor from the town of Bagley who had edited *Better Homes and Gardens* and *Ranger Rick* magazines. He was a gentle man who had learned to value all parts of the natural world and had learned how to interact with nature through his gardens, birdhouses, moth rearing, and dozens of other hobbies and experiences. On this walk on an unnamed island, we were in pursuit of a sound.

Dick had the ability to memorize bird songs, all the bird songs of North America, and this buzzy trill he identified as a blackburnian warbler. In those days, I knew very little about birds. We left the boat along the rocky shore and worked our way up a rocky slope, pushing through the brush, while the warbler sang contentedly from one perch.

When I think of all the bird courses I have taught in the years since this hike and all the frustrating bird adventures when I chased down a sound only to see the bird flit away from me the moment I located it, I am all the more fascinated by this hike. The bird kept calling to us, but when we got to the tree, I had the novice's eyes and could not separate the bird from the foliage. Dick was patient. "Look," he would say, and he would give me patient directions until finally my eye caught the bird sitting in the open, bill up, song warbling from its throat. "Wow, it's beautiful." My words were not profound, but then they seldom are when I am mesmerized by a new species or experience. I stood quietly watching and listening, and Dick leaned over to me. "Describe what you see. How does the bird look to you?"

I attempted to say what this small warbler looked like, but Dick wanted more. "Tell me about the chest. How does the orange look?" It seemed a strange request, but I grappled with my mental images and tried to describe the fiery glow of the orange, the way light seemed to emanate from the breast, how the throat seemed to stand out separately from the bird, and that it seemed incandescent. He smiled, this large man with the great love of birds, thanked me, and said, "You know, I'm color-blind. I can't see the glow you describe, but this is one of my favorite birds and I enjoyed hearing how you see it." That was the event that made me a bird watcher, lister, observer, bander, and teacher. Dick is gone now, a victim of cancer. His home is now a church retreat, but he is alive to me every spring when the blackburnian warbler sings.

(R. Miles)

ROCKS AND LICHENS

BY MIKE LINK

The rocks of canoe country are significant to all paddlers. They set the tone for the paddle. At times, the rocks tower overhead, dwarfing the paddler from their lofty heights, while on another lake, the rocks seem to be gone, until the keel slides onto a giant lurking beneath the water and reaching from the depths. Rocks attract us for swimming and sunbathing, for lunch stops, and as havens from biting insects. The rocks are more than remnants of Precambrian time or glacial sculpturing. They represent our human idea of permanence and strength. Their size, shape, and structure are fascinating, and the colors of the pink granites, greenstones, and dark gabbros contrast with sky, lake, and forest to paint pictures on the lake's reflective surface.

In the Saganaga and Seagull lakes area, a pink granitic rock dominates the islands and shoreline. It is a rock that formed beneath the surface and contains quartz aggregates, marble-size accumulations of quartz that are circular in shape. This is special rock, found nowhere else. It is part of the story of the earth, of molten magma, of old mountainous uplift, melting, and freezing. Nearby are other spectacular rocks that inspire geologists and carry their imaginations back billions of years.

Along the Gunflint Trail, an iron formation, banded and oxidized, sits as a road cut. It is ancient rock, a concentration of chert and iron that eroded from ancient landforms and collected in an early sea. Nearby is a trail to the magnet rocks, magnatite. The trail winds through the boreal landscape and ends at a large rock sculpted from the landscape by the last glacier.

There is a sense of monument about these rocks, something dramatic and mystic. They affect the compass and render it unusable in this area. A look at the lines on the topographic maps attest to the geographical confusion. The township and range lines waver in and out, creating sections of unequal distribution. These were set by early surveyors who didn't have airplanes or nonmagnetic survey devices.

West of Saganaga in the Knife Lake area, a conglomerate rock dominates the cliffs. Rocks inbedded in rocks are perched in horizontal layers. These were cobblestone beaches when the land of Saganaga was higher and eroding into ancient seas. The action is stopped, held in a timeless form that weaves a story for those who pause and ponder.

Duluth gabbro is the dark rock of canoe country, an intrusive rock filled with large crystals like a granite, but with crystals that are all dark minerals. These are the rocks that make the most dramatic cliffs. They represent a time when our continent was just forming, a time when it nearly split in two and a large rift extended from the BWCAW to Wichita, Kansas. Lava from a chamber beneath the present Lake Superior spilled out of the crack and made up the surface lavas near the shore. Then as these lavas cooled and plugged the rift, another surge of magma squirted beneath the surface to form a series of large gabbro sills.

As I canoe beneath this scenery, I absorb more than beauty, I also learn perspective.

The early canoeists must have seen more than rock, too, or they would not have been inspired to leave paintings on the sides of the cliffs. It was no idle thought that put the graffiti on the rock. And it wasn't done with a spray can, but with a mixture of red ochre and fish oil that was mixed together to create a permanent record. An ancient voice was placed on the rock.

The rocks hold other artwork as well, artwork that varies over the centuries with growth and competition. It is the design of the lichens, hardy pioneer plants that tenuously survive on seemingly impenetrable rock. Lichen comes in many forms. There is a crustose type that is imbedded in the rock, its phenol acid etching the surface in a way that allows the plant to grow intertwined with the crystalline structure. These are sometimes called coin lichens for the concentric growth pattern. The common ones in the BWCAW are grey and greenish.

The most exotic group is the fruticose lichens, a

(R. Miles)

39

group with fruiting bodies that mimic the fungus within the lichen. Lichens are a partnership that is sometimes called a symbiotic relationship. Two plants are united as one. There is a simple algae that can reproduce by splitting and can provide food by photosynthesis. Because the algae would dry up and die or slide off the face of the rock, a fungus part of the lichen has little threads that can grip the rock. The rock then deteriorates under the solution of phenol acid the fungus releases. The fungus can hold on, and it can form a hard exterior skin with a spongelike center that can hold water. It cannot make food, however, and the rock has no food to give. Therefore, the lichen must depend on its algae part for sustenance.

The shape of these lichens depends on the form of the mushroom that the fungus would produce if it were independent. We find light grey reindeer lichens, light green forked lichens, funnel-shaped pixie cup lichens, organ pipe, ladder, awl, deformed, and numerous other lichen variations. The most colorful is the British soldier, which resembles match sticks with red heads (coats). All of these were the food of the caribou. They grow under jack pines and on open rock slabs. They are pioneer plants and old forest

plants. Variations of this type hang from trees as old-man's-beard, a lichen that the parula warbler weaves into a nest.

The third type of lichen is foliose, a leafy plant form. One group is the umbilicates, with single large, leathery leaves that are attached to the rock by a group of fungal threads that are clustered in one umbilical mass. These are the tripes. Most large, vertical rock faces have them. They come in brown and grey, with the grey ones looking like elephant ears when they are wet and pliable.

The other foliose group forms shields, round rosettes of green, grey, yellow, and orange. They dominate the rocks of the canoe country, especially the bright, reddish orange rock lichen. Like the rock pictographs, this reddish orange coloration reaches along the cliff faces toward the water, where its reflection stretches like a train across the mirrorlike lake.

The colors of the lichen are bold, and they are set off by the dark forest above and the rocks that support the growth. No plant says canoe country more to me than this one, no plant represents the struggle against the demands of the north country more than the lichen, and none brings the land more cheer.

(R. Miles)

Pictographs painted on a rock wall by early residents of the BWCAW. A mixture of natural dyes and oils produced these long-lasting pictures. (D. Cox)

RIVERS

BY MIKE LINK

Canoe country is not all lakes. The Vermilion River in the west and the Granite River in the east are as wild and scenic as any that have been designated as such. Rainy and Pigeon rivers form the border and the backbone of the BWCAW. They flow with high energy over waterfalls and through rapids and widen to form lakes and quiet waters. North Shore streams carve through canyons of volcanic rock, and the Frost River dissects the glacial deposits above Cherokee Lake.

A love of rivers often begins in the fast places where foam and spray break the sunshine into a thousand little rainbows. But soon the edges where green and blue herons stalk become just as fascinating as chutes, eddies, and haystacks.

In the calm waters along the Kawishiwi, the currents are slowed by a reduced gradient and a wide course. Here the river becomes more like a lake or marsh, with shores extended by wet meadows of sweetgale, sedge, leatherleaf, and Labrador tea. Here red-winged blackbirds call their *conk-a-ree* from wind-bent reeds, and painted turtles bask in the sun on logs that are partially buried by river sediments.

The wet meadows hide secretive rails, the shyest of our bird families. The Virginia rail, which is a patchwork of stripes, and the black-faced, yellow-billed sora rail imitate the snipe's sky dance with ascending notes rather than with flight. These aquatic chickens move easily within the shallow water areas and prefer to run rather than fly.

Ducks find places to hide between the wild rice stalks, and black ducks and wood ducks conceal their young in hidden runways. Northern pike spawn in the grassy sections.

The canoe moves sluggishly over the soft, organic bottom of very shallow places. Paddles loosen bubbles of gas from the partial decomposition. These areas will fill up with organic matter and become communities known as shrub bars. Speckled alder and willow will dominate these old stream beds.

The shallow pools between the rapids are the nutrient banks of the river, the gardens of organic matter to support the life that is more uniquely stream oriented. It is the pool that feeds the rapids, just as the pool regenerates the energy of the paddler before the drop.

As the current gains momentum, ribbons of floating leaf bur reed point downstream and net-weaving caddis flies anchor themselves on the underwater stems. The caddis fly is a terrestrial adult, but most of its life is spent as an aquatic juvenile, with each species developing its own special way of finding food in the fast-moving current.

Because the young are light and soft bodied, they require an anchored existence to prevent them from being dashed on the rocks and yet allow them to eat. The group known as net weavers secretes a substance that attaches them to the vegetation, and then they weave this glue into a mesh of net that resembles an airsock, with the wide end facing upstream so that the current holds it open. The sock narrows like a cornucopia as it curls under into a narrow foot where the larvae can rest and wait for organic matter from the pools to be swept into the seine.

In the faster riffles, the caddis fly's net would be damaged by the turbulence of the current, so the species that reside here glue bits of stone together to form cones in which they can live. As they grow, they merely add another wider ring of stone to the cones, and their houses grow as they do. This cover is not only unpalatable to predators, but it is also ballast to keep the larvae from drifting downstream.

Surprisingly, the concentration of organisms most peculiar to streams is found in the rapids. These bastions of fury are also the quiet waters of small life. The myriad stones and rocks that alter the calmness of the surface also deflect the bottom waters into hundreds of small eddies that interact to calm the stream's turbulence and almost halt the current within the miniature canyons and peaks of the landscape below the white water.

Waters from the lakes of the Arrowhead Trail form the Pigeon River. Waterfalls such as this one caused the creation of the nine-mile "grand portage." (R. Morreim)

(R. Morreim)

(S. Kuchera)

44

(R. Morreim)

Where the river slows and widens, marsh plants like the wild purple iris grow. (D. Cox)

Riffle beetles are well adapted to the current. Their larvae are oval and streamlined to confront the current head on. Called water pennies, these young have a body that overlaps their legs and head and sags around them, creating a suction that holds them on the rock. The water penny is a thin suction cup with all its organs and legs inside. Its protective covering provides the animal with peace while it harvests the plant life of the rapids.

The rapids are too strong for water hemlock and the other flowering plants of calm water. They would be bent and broken by the current. But there is life here. There are algae, like the red *Lemanea* that grows only in rapids and falls or the green algae *Cladophora*. Some algae have holdfasts that cling to the rocks, and others have an abundance of mucous secretion that encases the cells and seals them to the rocks. The microscopic desmids live in a world that is beyond our experience. It is a world of floating and drifting, so free and light that the mere surface of a rock is such a force of friction that the desmid sticks to it rather than flowing with the current. The rocks are often covered with thousands of desmids or mucous-secreting algaes, and canoists slip and bang their shins when they try to walk their canoes through these areas.

The froth that is white water is a whipped mass of gas and liquid, water and air. This oxygen-rich environment is less dense and less stable than normal water. It is here that the kayaker can paddle a submerged boat, because it is less buoyant in the lighter foam. It is here that the water of the river takes on its oxygen load and purifies itself.

The animals of the rapids depend on this oxygen richness for their survival. If the stone fly's search for food takes it too far from the main oxygenated water, it will pause and do "push-ups" to increase the flow of water through its gills.

Pulsating black masses line the walls of the northern waterfalls — millions of blackfly larvae attached to the wet, slippery rock face. Attachment is frequently the key to survival in this aquatic world. The blackfly larvae reside in the fastest waters because they need the oxygen of falls and rapids. When they become alarmed, they drift downstream and then, when the coast is clear, return via a thread that has been spun from the rock. Unlike the midge and stone fly, the blackfly emerges in fast, full streams. When they have reached maturity, the back of the larvae casing splits and an air bubble emerges with the adult. It floats to the surface, dissipates, and the adult flies away.

Fly fishermen know that a good lure placed in the current just at the edge of the rapids and allowed to float into the pool beneath is a good way to catch a hungry trout. Fish line up beneath the rocks, with their heads toward the current. The water breaks gently, flows around them, and forms eddies behind their tails, allowing them to wait without effort.

The trout are waiting there because, inevitably, something will happen to the otherwise secure rapid's life, and the organisms that live there will be cast into the current and sent downstream. Those who study the river life call this drift material. Drift material is life caught in a maelstrom of current and can be generated by a curious naturalist overturning a rock, a surge of water from a storm or dam opening, or a rolled rock caught on the keel of a canoe. Underwater, the surge of energy is sudden and strong, and life is ripped from its hold in a chaotic moment of disorientation. The eddies are overwhelmed, the miniature canyons feel pulses of current, like flash floods, and those organisms caught in the fury are swept into the pool below and the net of fish mouths that wait for such a moment.

The river seems to lose some of its width as willows and alders lean out to reach the sunlight between the shores. They secure the shore from the cutting power of the current and in the summer support the warblers and flycatchers that feed on the emerging insects. It is in this zone that the kingfisher ties the land and the water together, nesting in the ground, hunting from the branches, and taking its food from the water with a quick flight and the stab of its beak. Kingfishers move downstream from the paddler, rattling and diving as though sewing land and water together with stitches that reach from branch to water and back to branch again.

Seasons pass and so do years. Bloodroot and marsh marigold lead to boneset and joe-pye weed, running waters give way to oceans, adult insects emerge and return to lay eggs, and life derives energy from death. There is always change, but there is also continuity, and the river reflects the health of the planet and the joys of discovery.

Oriental philosophy draws many parallels between the river and life, from its small beginnings to its slow and ponderous end, with rocky spots and smooth stretches in between. The river is a symbolic organism of strength and moods (floods), changes and adjustments (oxbows), growing with each new encounter (confluence) to become the sum of all its experiences before pouring them into the collective knowledge of the planet (the oceans).

For those of us seeking the essence of the river, there are many ways to experience its breadth and length. To those who would know the river best, the experience must be both physical and intellectual, for the sum of the two is wisdom. The river is the naturalist's highway.

Overleaf: Cliff overlooking the Kawishiwi River.
(D. Cox)

47

In quiet water, whirligig beetles will lay their eggs on the undersides of lily-pad leaves. (P. and J. Sublett)

SMALL
AND SIGNIFICANT

BY KATE CROWLEY

When you first arrive in the Boundary Waters, you are full of anticipation, eager to absorb the majestic beauty and magnificent silence of the area. In the beginning, your eyes only see nature on a grand scale — large, wave-capped lakes, immense slabs of dark rock rising from the waters, age-old pines reaching high into the sky. It can overwhelm you and make you feel small and insignificant.

Gradually, as you relax and become one with this ancient world, you slow down enough to see the smaller miracles. A few minutes spent sitting on a rock near some quiet water can bring you discoveries and memories as important as any gained through solitude. For there are creatures that live in the Boundary Waters that receive none of the sensational attention of the wolves and loons — creatures just as fascinating, only smaller. They live in and around the water. They are carnivores and predators like the wolves, depend on the water for their survival like the loons, and are just as important to the aesthetic appeal and ecological balance of the area.

WHIRLIGIGS

I sat along the river's edge and watched the water beetles react en masse to changes in the surrounding water. The mere sprinkle of water droplets or the soft landing of a yellowed maple leaf was frightening enough to send members of the "flock" darting off in opposite directions. If, however, a small insect had dropped into the water, I would have witnessed a much different response in the whirligigs. They are predators and, as such, react quickly to the special vibrations created by the helpless flapping or struggling of a fly caught in the surface film. This creates a response in the beetles comparable to the ringing of the dinner bell at a boy scout camp. The whirligigs zero in and quickly devour their prey.

The special apparatus needed for such sensitivity to vibration is found in the whirligigs' two antennae, which project out from their heads and touch the water surface. The apparatus is called Johnston's organ and involves a complex arrangement of tactile hairs. Because of this special adaptation, the whirligig beetles can swim in close quarters and never collide with one another. Their own movement creates vibrations that bounce off other objects in the water and back to them, a process similar to echolocation used by bats.

Normally, when we see whirligigs, they are responding to our approach because of our paddles dipping and dripping into the water. With the aid of a breeze or current, it is possible to drift close to them on a warm summer day and find them basking on logs or rocks like lazy turtles.

As I watched them in the small eddy of the river on a warm Indian summer afternoon, their activity was appropriately relaxed. When left undisturbed, they would drift back with the current or move forward with slow and somewhat jerky progress. Their two pairs of flattened, hairy hind legs were almost hidden under their oval bodies. These paddlelike legs propel the beetle in a coordinated sculling motion that can switch in a moment from lazy paddling to eye-snapping, erratic spurts across the surface. Some species even have a keel-shaped ventral side, which allows them to slip through the water with even greater ease.

If I stood and moved to another location, the beetles would dart out toward the swift main current of the river, but they would turn back to the safety of the eddy before the pull of the rushing water could capture and sweep them away. Whirligigs are able to see as well as feel movement, with eyes that are divided at the midline of the body. The upper portion of the eyes can scan the water and shoreline for danger, while the lower half are pressed against the water surface to watch for predators. This arrangement may also help the female search for an appropriate place to lay her eggs — often on the underside of a pondweed or lily-pad leaf.

Each spring, as soon as the ice begins to leave the

lakes and rivers, the whirligigs reappear. They stay close to the shorelines and backwaters to begin with, but move out into more open water as the season progresses. They will swirl on the surface waters until their liquid playground hardens to a shell of ice. Through the long winters, they hibernate in the mud, sometimes emerging during a midwinter thaw for a brief spin on the surface, then submerging again as the ice returns.

Whirligigs can dive beneath the surface, and when they do, they carry a bubble of air under their body to use as a scuba diver uses an oxygen tank. The whirligig has a distinct advantage over the scuba diver, because as its oxygen is depleted from the bubble, oxygen from the surrounding water passes into the bubble and resupplies the insect during its dive.

The whirligig is even able to fly if it finds a launching spot out of the water, but its real realm is the water surface. Look closely at a group of whirligigs and you will see a depression beneath them. They do not break through the film but press down on it, as your finger would depress the skin of an inflated balloon.

Imagine being able to travel on top of the water, to be able to zip from one place to another and never create so much as a microscopic splash. We know the feeling of lightness that floating in water gives our bodies. What must it feel like to be supported by the taut, uppermost molecular layer of water?

Most of the field guides describe the whirligigs as being flat, but the species I have observed, gyrinus, has a distinctive convex back. To sit and watch a swarm of whirligig beetles is hypnotic. Their blue-black bodies reflect the sun in such a way that at certain angles they appear to be bubbles risen to the surface. They swim idly about, zigging and zagging as the mood suits them. Every once in awhile, one may spin wildly on its own axis, a behavior that has earned them the name whirligig, or the scientific name Gyrinidae. Like most creatures that people have watched and wondered about, the whirligig has accumulated a collection of common names based on its behavior: submarine chasers, lucky bugs, dizzy bugs, write-my-names, and, my favorite, administrator beetles.

WATER STRIDERS

On top of a glass-smooth puddle of water near a rocky island edge, there is a skating exhibition taking place. The participants glide gracefully and noiselessly from one shady edge to the other. Try to approach closer to get a better look and the skaters are gone, fleeing to the deeper shadows and behind rocks.

Sometimes there is no escape or your approach is unnoticed; then you can watch the long-legged, spiderlike water striders perform their magic. Like the whirligigs, these insects inhabit the thin, skinlike layer where water meets air. They too will scatter with any frightening disturbance on the water surface, rejoining and gradually reappearing when the danger is past. If necessary, they will even leap from the water and go jumping across land until they reach the safety of another puddle.

They too are predators and carnivores. The front pair of legs are held up, poised to seize any unfortunate insect that falls and becomes trapped by the surface tension. Unlike the whirligig, the water strider uses its eyes to locate its prey. When an insect struggles to free itself from the water, its legs thrash and reflect light, glittering like gold to the strider. It races over, grasps the prey, inserts its beaklike mouth into the victim, and consumes it. Water striders will also act as scavengers, eating dead insects that drift by as they scoot from here to there (another one of nature's clean-up crews). The strider is not confined to food found floating by; it is also capable of jumping into the air to snatch a low-flying insect. Is it possible that the surface tension gives the strider an extra boost and bounce, like a trampoline?

Sometimes, if the light is just right, you don't see the insect itself, just its enlarged shadow moving across the sunny, sandy bottom of a shallow pool. Where its four legs touch the surface of the water, there are four dark round shadows—mirrors of the dimples that are created by the feet.

The legs and underside of the body are covered with fine, water-repellent hair, which allows the insect to skate, slide, and stride across a body of water. This seemingly miraculous ability to walk on water has led some people in Texas to bestow on the water strider the name "Jesus bug." By standing splay-legged on the water, they can disperse their body weight to facilitate their surface-striding lifestyle. Watch closely and you'll see that a water strider uses the middle pair of legs, its longest, to push itself forward, while the rear pair of legs act as a rudder to steer from behind. There are tarsal claws on the ends of the legs, but these are set far back from the tip in order to prevent an accidental puncture of the surface film. To pierce the surface layer could lead to disaster. While some water striders are able to envelop their bodies with a layer of air for brief submersion, the majority are very susceptible to drowning. A curling wave or paddle splash near a strider can douse it and drag it under. Its only hope, then, is to find something dry to climb onto, where it will wait until it is dry once again.

The water strider is an insect that spends the nicest months of the year skimming over and around crystal clear water, moving with what appears to be so little effort, and living a carefree life. Even fish leave them alone because of a special repellent they can secrete.

The closest we humans can come to the water strider's lifestyle is to wait until the coldest months of the year, when the surface water layer becomes ice. Then we must cover ourselves with endless layers of clothing, tie on some shoes with sharpened blades on the soles, and attempt to stand on the hardened water. With time and practice, some of us may even learn to glide and stride over the glazed surface and feel exhilarated as the scenery flashes by and an icy wind hits our face. But it just takes one small crack in the ice, one little miscalculation of our inner ear, and down we go, arms and legs flying in all directions to land with a thud that bruises our egos as well as our bodies.

And somewhere down below us, under the ice and snow, wait the most graceful skaters of all. Luckily, they are well hidden under rocks and sticks and cannot witness our clumsy, lumbering attempts to imitate their light-footed, tiptoe perambulations of the warm summer months.

DRAGONFLIES

While paddling across Lake Jeannette on a hot, sunny August afternoon, a big green darner—the largest of the dragonflies—flew across the bow of the canoe, turned, and landed on my knee. I held my breath, afraid that it would soon realize it had made a tactical error on landing and lift off before I had a chance to imprint its beautiful shining image on my brain. It must have needed a rest, for it continued to cling to my skin. I bent nearer and marveled at its translucent wings and bulbous eyes. Though I could not feel its feet grasping my skin, it had a good enough grip to hang on, even as I resumed paddling. Every once in awhile, it would flutter its wings, as if to maintain its balance. Finally, as I knew it must, it let go and swiftly flew away. I felt as fortunate as if a fragile, flight-weary bird had chosen me for a resting place.

The things that I find exquisitely beautiful and fascinating about dragonflies are the same things that cause immediate horror in others. Over the years, I've had many opportunities to closely observe and study these insects and have come to realize that they are harmless to humans, and sometimes downright docile. Still, it is easy to understand why so many people on first encountering dragonflies or their smaller cousins, damselflies, react with such strong apprehension. Their appearance is menacing. Huge, bulging eyes cover most of the head. Six black, spiny legs hang in a cluster just beneath the thorax. A set of four large, whirring wings stick straight out from a long, segmented, slender body (up to 3½ inches long), and at the end of the body, there may be a dangerous looking pair of pincers.

Like many other misunderstood creatures, dragonflies have accumulated some scary names and powers well beyond their means. It was not uncommon in the past to threaten naughty little boys by saying that the devil's darning needles (darner dragonflies) would sew up their ears or mouths if they didn't behave. Some called them snake doctors and snake feeders, believing they ministered to the needs of the reptiles. This association may have been based on the dragonfly's long, narrow body, which appears to be protected by platelike scales. Still others called them horse stingers, believing they used the grasping pincers found on the male's body as stingers.

Other insects have good reason to fear these flying predators, and humans should be happy to see members of the order Odonata, for a large portion of their diet consists of mosquitoes. In fact, another common name for the dragonfly is mosquito hawk. I watched a squadron of dragonfly silhouettes zooming over the tall grasses at the Lake Jeannette campsite. The sun had just set, the sky was a pale grey-blue, and you could almost hear the mosquitoes rising in full force. This was the cue for the dragonflies. Like phantom jets, they streaked back and forth, scooping up the buzzing, blood-sucking pests. I cheered them on.

I did wonder how they saw their prey in such dim light, but apparently with their large, compound eyes, they were able to gather the available light and create a mosaic vision adequate to their task. Their eyes are actually many eyes in one—as many as 10,000 to 20,000 components, called ommatidia, are packed together in a honeycomblike cluster. They come in a rainbow of colors—varying shades of blue, green, orange, yellow, red, brown, and black. I once saw a small dragonfly perched on a rock at midday, and as I looked closer, I saw a white dot in the center of each golden eye. Bending still closer, I discovered it was a dual reflection of the shining sun. Even though it lacks eyelids, somehow the insect's retinal rods are protected from direct sunlight.

I have looked at the many-faceted eyes of dragonflies by inverting a pair of binoculars. Placing the small eyepiece near the insect and looking through the wide end produces a strong magnification. Of course, you need a complacent, cooperative insect to do this, but occasionally that will happen on cool mornings, when the dragonfly's body temperature is too low to allow it to rev up its wings and take off.

The fragile-looking wings of the dragonfly and damselfly are crystal clear, with a network of veins that provide shape and strength. One of the ways to tell a damselfly from a dragonfly is to look at the wings. The damselfly has two pairs of wings attached to the body with a narrow base, which allows the wings to be folded parallel to the body when at rest. Dragonfly wings have broader bases, and the hind wing is slightly wider than the forewing. These wings are perpetually extended at right angles to the body. If you could see a dragonfly flying in slow motion, you'd see the front pair of wings going up while the hind pair was going down. In some, this is very pronounced. In others, the front wings may be moving only slightly ahead of the hind wings. In either case, during flight the wings are a blur to our eyes. Dragonflies are the fastest flying insects.

I came across a dragonfly whose wings had seen better days. It was clinging to a dark rock. Its wings were a dull grey rather than the normal sparkling see-through silver, and there were pieces missing. I didn't expect it had much longer to live. Dragonfly adults may last six to eight weeks, while their smaller relatives, the damselflies, probably live as adults for only three to four weeks.

We normally don't see them during the early stages of life, when they live in the water as nymphs. In the last stages of development, the nymph crawls up out of the water on a slender stalk of pond vegetation. The exoskeleton dries, and like a suit coat grown too tight,

it slowly begins to split down the back. The pale, soft-bodied, and limp-winged adult gradually steps out of its old skin and clings to the nearest surface. It begins to pump fluid into its wings, and they expand and take shape. Disaster can still strike. Sometimes there are many dragonflies emerging at the same time and in the same area. If the insect is too close to another that is also going through this process, a wing may be blocked from expanding to its full size and thus shape and harden into a deformed, useless appendage. If nothing impedes the wing development, within a half hour they are fully expanded and the dragonfly flies weakly away. It will be a few days before it is able to fly at full power and maybe a week or two before it has developed its full color.

The velvety reds, metallic blues, and brilliant greens of the dragonflies are the kind of striking colors you expect to see on exotic butterflies. One color is described as Tyndall blue—the bright blue of a clear sky—and it is achieved in much the same way. Like the dust particles in the atmosphere that separate us from an infinity of blackness beyond, there are fine particles on the black cuticle of the dragonfly's body that shatter the light hitting them, thus creating the color blue. The green dragonflies have an extra, thin covering of yellow pigments over the blue, which then creates a green coloration.

It is in the warm summer months that we see the largest concentration of dragonflies. Over fields of grass and wildflowers, along stream edges, on cattails in marshes and ponds, their whirring wings can be heard. They search the skies for other flying insects that they can capture in their grasping front legs.

Once caught, their prey is carried in a basketlike structure just under their thorax, formed by the legs. In this manner, they transport their meal to a suitable spot for a picnic, or they can eat while on the go, just by bending their head down to the food held below.

But summer is not just spent flying and feeding. A more important task needs to be accomplished—the continuation of the species. Dragonflies do not over-winter as adults. Eggs must be laid to ensure another generation. When you see a pair of damselflies or dragonflies flying in tandem—one towing another by means of the tail pincers—you are witnessing pre- or post-copulatory behavior. The male uses his pincers to grab and clasp the female of his choice behind her head. Copulation can take place while in flight or while perched on a slender stem. The female curls her abdomen forward until the tip touches the second segment of the male's body, where she receives the sperm. After the eggs have been fertilized, the pair may remain joined while the female lays her eggs in water or plant tissue. Or they may separate, in which case, the male will often stand guard as the female deposits the eggs. An unprotected female is an easy target for another amorous male, who can easily swoop down and carry her away with her egg laying left unfinished.

The cycle of life goes on, and the following summer another crop of dazzling dragonflies will take to the air as they have for millions of years. According to the fossil record, there once was a dragonfly that had a wingspan of more than two feet. Even I might be a little nervous with one of those buzzing by.

A storm brewed near Lake Jeannnette but dissipated by sunset, when dragonflies took to the air and their nightly hunt. (K. Crowley)

Yellow lady's slipper (D. Cox)

PLANT LIFE

BY MIKE LINK

The flowers of canoe country have a special flair to them. They are different from the woodland flowers of spring. In the boreal forest, most of the trees retain their foliage, so the plants do not get a solar advantage for quick growth and early flower formation. The woodland flowers live in coolness, and they take on forms that have a more complex development.

ORCHIDS

Worldwide, the orchid family rivals the daisy family for the largest number of species. They are abundant and associated with the tropical forests, but they are also important in the boreal complex, where the plants range from the showy lady's slippers to the more inconspicuous green bog orchids and plantains.

These plants are slow growing, with some of the lady's slippers taking as many as twenty years to grow from a seed to a seed producer. The flowers of the orchid family stand out because of their symmetry. In the lady's slipper, the bulbous lip, or pouch, is as conspicuous as the lower petal and its two lateral companions. In other orchids, the pouch is not present. The lower petal is always present, and it may be fringed or enlarged. This lower petal is deceptive. In most of our orchids, if we were to watch the twisting growth of the plant, we would observe that the plant actually turns on its stalk, and the lower lip is really the upper.

The center of the orchid is unusual too. It does not have the normal alignment of stigmas and styles but a column of style, stigma, and stamens joined together in a colorful arrangement. In the lady's slipper, there are two fertile stamens that produce sticky disks that adhere to feeding bees and a third sterile stamen that forms a scraper for the removal of disks from other flowers.

The genus of the lady's slippers is *Cypripedium*, a word that means the sandal of Aphrodite. In canoe country we have the pink, showy, and yellow lady's slippers.

The earliest forms of orchids include the *Arethusa*, or swamp-pink, a pink flower that seems to cascade from a leafless stem (legend says that Arethusa was changed into a spring to escape the river god), and the coralroots of the genus *Corallorhiza*. The coralroots are flower versions of mushrooms, plants with no green chlorophyll that support themselves by living on dead matter in the soil. They have scales on their branches instead of leaves. The plants have racemes of flowers and are named for the decoration on their lower petals—spots or stripes.

There are many other groups of orchids, but the one that sticks out in my observations is the rattlesnake plantains. On an August portage, where the trail leaves the lakeshore and moves inland, certain rose-colored leaves along the trail may have a short stalk of inconspicuous flowers. The leaves are similar to the common plantain plants that line the borders of sidewalks and driveways, but they are in no way related. The leaves are decorated with white lines that form networks and patterns along the midrib or outer leaf edge.

The leaves are beautiful works of art and far exceed the flowers as attention grabbers. They were named rattlesnake plantains because the vein network resembled snake skin, and it was believed that the leaves could be chewed for protection against the rattler. It works in canoe country, but only because there are no rattlesnakes there.

PYROLAS

This woodland flower family may be found in abundance in some parts of the forest. Their flower and form make them memorable, but insects tend to make midsummer explorers stay out of the forest unless they have a canoe over their head and they are hurrying from one lake to another. There are two forms of this family, one with dark green waxy leaves and one without green color, a saprophitic (living off decaying matter) group.

Rose pagonia is an orchid often found in open, wet meadows and sphagnum bogs. It is the first to perish when bogs begin to dry. (S. Eaton)

The pipsissewas have waxy leaves growing up their branches. The leaves stay green all winter under the snow and produce food as soon as the spring sun hits them. Most of the plant is underground, and the portion we see is a branch of a stem that grows along the surface and is usually covered by humus. They are also called love-in-winter and prince's pine, a name that is sure to be confused with the princess pine, a green club moss that covers large areas of the forest floor. The pipsissewa leaves are used as a flavoring in root beer and have a pleasant flavor when chewed.

The shinleafs are very similar plants, but their leaves are clustered near the ground. They were called shinleafs because the leaves were used in plasters to treat shin injuries.

The second group of Pyrolaceae includes the Indian pipe, sweet pinesap, pinesap, and pinedrops. All of these plants live off decaying matter and are found in the forest. The most common is the Indian pipe. It is flesh colored (another common name is corpse plant) and flowers with a drooping bloom that gives it a pipe appearance. As it matures to seed, the stalk straightens out and turns black.

BOG PLANTS

The canoe country is divided into many plant combinations, which ecologists refer to as plant communities. There are communities dominated by the pines—red, jack, and white; there are communities of northern hardwoods—birch and aspen (hardwoods like oak and maple are in old forested areas); and there are watery communities like cedar and ash swamps, wild rice beds, *Phragmites* stands, sedge meadows, and lily beds. But the community that best describes the boreal ecology is the bog.

Bogs are dominated by sphagnum, a moss that grows to phenomenal lengths and concentrations. It absorbs ten times its own weight in water, and it floats. Sphagnum is more than a plant of the bog, it is a growing medium as well. The water of a bog is highly acidic, sometimes too acidic for much life to exist in, except for the sphagnum, so this plant forms a floating mass on which other plants can grow.

The surface sphagnum traps fresh rainwater, a nonacidic water that can support other plant forms, and it gives the other plants a thick organic base for root development. The plants that grow here have a uniqueness that matches the community's limitations. There are leaves that are waxy, leaves that are covered with scales, leaves with fuzzy concentrations of plant hairs, and leaves that roll their edges. All of these adaptations can be found in another community—the desert. They are meant to prevent water loss from the plant, to conserve water budgets, and to keep the

plant alive. In this watery environment, these plant adaptations prevent the absorption of too much highly acidic water, which would destroy the plant tissues.

Bog plants have limited nitrogen available to them. To offset this, some of the plants have turned to insects for both pollination and food. The pitcher plant has fused leaves that trap fresh water and the insects that are looking for it. The pitcher has attractive nectar glands just above the waterline and a shape that makes escape nearly impossible. If the insect decides to climb out, the downward-pointing hairs form a discouraging sequence of overhangs. In the water, an enzyme breaks down the insect and releases the nitrogen to the plant.

In sundew, the leaves have another adaptation. They are shaped like spoons or spatulas with short, translucent hairs. Each hair exudes a droplet of "dew," which is sweet tasting and sticky. An insect with an attraction to sweets soon finds itself stuck on its lunch and struggles to get free. The struggle is useless, except that the vibrations stimulate a hormone release that causes the outside half of the hairs to grow rapidly. Since the tension of the nongrowing half is toward the center of the leaf, the hair bends inward and the insect is caught in a closed cage. An enzyme is released that dissolves the insect's soft tissues, and the plant feeds. Then, with the new nitrogen, the plant releases a second hormone that causes the insides of the hair to grow to a matching length, straightening out the plant hairs and ejecting the exoskeletal remains of the insect.

Most of the bog plants are woody plants that grow year after year so that slow rates of growth can be made up by longevity. The tops of black spruce are thick, condensed congregations of many decades of growth. The black spruce augments this slow upward growth by forming new trees from its lower branches (layering). As the sphagnum grows, the plants on its surface must have a way to escape suffocation. In the spruce, the lower branches bend upward at the tips, the midsection develops roots within the buried section, and the large tree is surrounded by a circle of clones.

Other plants grow adventitious roots, new roots that extend from the stalk just at the surface, or they spread by runners that quickly disappear in the moss. The bog is an interrelated community because of the connections between individuals as well as the sphagnum. The forest responds in waves to disturbance. As the wind bends trees on one side of the bog, their movement ripples through the sphagnum and ends in ripples on the other side. Human steps also send waves of energy through the bog, and our movements ripple through the treetops like concentric rings on the surface of the water.

Gray jay (D. Cox)

GRAY JAYS & LOONS

BY KATE CROWLEY

MIKE LINK

GRAY JAYS

Not long after you've set up your camp in the Boundary Waters, you can expect the arrival of the "official" welcoming party. Wearing a conservative suit of grey, a pair of *Perisoreus canadensis* silently alight on the picnic table or a nearby branch. They do not bring a welcoming basket of goodies, however. They prefer to confiscate any tasty morsel you leave unattended.

The common names for this bold bird are many and frequently descriptive of its larcenous habits and carnivorous tastes. It used to be known as the Canada jay, but it is common in the boreal forests of our northern states. It is also called whisky jack and camp robber. When food is within range, the gray jay will venture into human encampments, boldly entering tents and buildings. With patience and a tasty tidbit, it can even be coaxed to perch on an extended hand. Two observers once ran a test on the food preference of these birds and discovered that their favorite choices were cheese and baked beans—provisions that are generally in good supply at wilderness camps.

While the recreational camper finds the bravado of the gray jay entertaining, the trapper of old found them to be a serious nuisance to his line of work. A report from 1909 tells us, "Hunger is the chief characteristic of these docile birds and no potential food is refused . . . Meat of any sort has an especial attraction to them and they are the despair of the trapper because of their propensity for stealing bait." Their carnivorous tastes gave them the names meat-bird, grease-bird, and even butcher bird, for the habit of taking young from nests. John J. Audubon said they were called the carrion bird in Maine in the early 1800s because "when hungry, they shew no alarm at the approach of man, nay, become familiar, troublesome, and sometimes so very bold as to enter camps of the 'lumberers' or attend to rob them of bait affixed to their traps."

The gray jay belongs to the Corvidae family, which also includes the crows, magpies, and other jays. It is an omnivore, meaning it will eat meat or vegetable matter, whichever is easiest to get. Lacking table scraps, it feeds on small mammals, moth eggs, insects, berries, seeds (not hardshell, like sunflower seeds), mushrooms, and, in times of severe food shortage, lichens. Like the other Corvidae, the gray jay has a special throat pouch that can store and carry food. The gray jay also has enlarged salivary glands that aid in the production of a bolus (wad of food stuck together) to put in the pouch. This sticky ball of extra food is then carried by the jay to a tree, generally a conifer, and pressed into a fork in the branches or into a crevice, where it can be retrieved at a later time. Jays are very cautious and protective of their hiding places. Knowing the thieving habits of their fellow jays, they will either chase the intruder away or wait for it to leave and then remove the food and hide it again in a different place.

Gray jays in flight are as silent as owls. Gliding on outspread wings, they are grey shadows that drop out of the sky to the scene of the crime. Most often they will land, look around briefly, and then quickly bend forward and pick up the chow with their short, black bill. They have been known to carry away larger food items in their feet. On one winter camping trip, a man decided to capture, on film, the dusky bandit making off with the goods. He set a bait with his dinner, an eight-ounce piece of steak, which he believed to be more than the bird could possibly carry. Then, with camera poised, he sprawled out on the snow near the meat. The jay flew down as expected, took one look around, grabbed the meat, and flew away, leaving the photographer open mouthed, pictureless, and hungry.

Whenever I see gray jays casing out their next heist, they are traveling in pairs, one bird apparently dominant over the other. You can be sure that they will know of your presence before you know of theirs.

They are alert to sounds coming from a camp or the smoke rising from a campfire. You may hear a squeaky call or, more likely, a low chattering as they sweep into your clearing. They may land in the branches of a nearby conifer and hop from one branch to another before making their brazen entry. It is difficult to see them when they sit still in the pines, for their plumage blends well with the pale grey bark of the trees.

They are not flashy birds, but they brighten any camping trip by their bravery. They stay in the cold north woods through the long winters, when so many of their feathered relatives leave for warmer, less stressful climes. It is easy to imagine earlier campers in these boreal forests, wearing skins instead of polypropylene, using bark canoes instead of fiber glass, and being just as enchanted and amused by the feathered filcher, the gray jay.

LOONS

The September morning sun took effect slowly, mounting the ridgetop to the east of Pine Lake and slowly picking up the fog from the lake's surface. Our canoes moved quietly in the stillness, gliding almost effortlessly as each paddler worked to maintain the solitude. The fog stood as a curtain in front of our boats, and the sun penetrated it as a soft-edged globe. The rays from the sun were diffuse, and we could look right at it. It was a golden greyness, and the land had a primitive sensation that held us in awe. We were immersed in the wilderness.

The shoreline took shape slowly, with rocks glistening in the sunlight that slipped beneath the fog's skirt. Water rippled around the dark boulders, and our movement sent shivers of waves to lap at the cobblestone lake edge. A peninsula of trees suddenly turned gold as the sun backlit the aspens, and the glow spilled onto the water, where two birds swam.

These were loons, stocky in silhouette, low in the water, with large bills and large heads. They swam quietly too. Nothing seemed to want to disturb the morning. Their plumage lacked the summer contrast of black and white, but they were beautiful in a more graceful way, and we observed their shape rather than their pattern.

Their movement seemed to be in unison, and they were oblivious to us. We paused and stared. Then recognition. Perhaps a droplet from a paddle stirred them, and their reaction was instantaneous. We did not see them go under, we just realized that they were no longer there. Their exit had a haunting speed to it.

This is Minnesota's state bird, the common loon, a diving bird with the oldest lineage of all the birds in existence today. They are not ducks, geese, or grebes; they are a family of their own, with five species around the world. They nest in the northern fringe of the United States and across Canada, on lakes that are cold and clear and deep. They dive for their food, and they engage in a wide range of social behaviors that enliven the canoe country.

They call as they display and dance on the water's surface, a warning to us that we are too close and need to move away. They call in flight and when they greet each other. Their migrations take them to the oceans and salt water. Here the young will spend three years before returning north, but the adults come back as soon as the ice leaves.

They nest on islands, old beaver lodges, in the muskeg, and along the shore. The nest is sphagnum and mud, a shallow bowl with two eggs. They are lucky if one chick survives or even hatches. They are bothered by the curious bird lover, the recreationist who doesn't understand the stress he or she can cause when the bird is doing its "penguin dance." They are threatened by gulls, ravens, mink, otter, and other egg predators, by sterile waters from acid rain, and by predation from fish and turtles. The normal successful pair raises one young and then flies off, leaving the adolescent to discover its own route to the ocean.

The loon has become a symbol of wildness and of freedom. It is obvious, yet it is elusive. We can see the loons easily and therefore we think that the bird's population is okay, when in fact the success of its reproduction won't be evident for decades. Sometimes the very visibility of the bird, which has a lifespan of twenty-five years, causes us to overestimate its numbers.

A canoeist may be treated to loons diving beneath the boat, but don't plan on it. If you try to approach the bird, it will dive and disappear for long moments while you scan the horizon looking for it to come back up. The loon can control its buoyancy and may lift only its beak for air before descending again.

In the fog, our loons disappeared and left no trace, but we heard the call and thought to ourselves that it must have been the ones we saw. The calls are rollicking echoes in the lake country. The yodel rolls out of the bird's bill and rebounds in every bay. Its wail is eerie, and its tremolo is a vibration as well as a sound. The loon voice is part of the full moon and the aurora borealis, part myth, part reality. There are multiple dimensions to its sound, dimensions of emotion as well as vibrations and notes.

A canoe country without the loon would be dead and uninviting.

(R. Morreim)

Red squirrel (S. Kuchera)
Another small mammal of the boundary waters, the eastern chipmunk, is often seen scurrying on and around the rocky islands.
(D. Cox)

SMALL MAMMALS

BY MIKE LINK

SQUIRRELS

Beneath the bows of a spruce was a small reddish brown mound. It began near the trunk and sprawled away from the tree in a growing concentric pattern. It was a midden, an eating establishment for a red squirrel, who stood beneath the protecting canopy of branches and slowly took cones apart to separate the edible seed from the inedible scales. The squirrel had obviously been using this spot for a lot of eating in this season, for the mound was over two feet high.

Squirrels are the woodland gatherers, the spunky reddish mammals that dart from branch to branch and add their chorus to the other calls of the woodlands. They chatter and flick their tails while bounding on stiff front legs; they cluck and squeak, chip and rattle. They call to each other, warn the woods of intruders, confront, signal, converse, and play. They are our version of a woodland imp.

We watch them dart around our camps and stand eye to eye with them as they scold us from the tree trunk. We see other animals respond to their warnings, and we watch the interactions of their courtship chases, territorial defenses, and family interactions.

The squirrel is also important for the forest ecology. It is the planter and the sower. In the oak forests, the grey squirrel buries acorns. In the conifer forest, the red squirrel is just as important.

The squirrel enjoys the seeds of the various conifers, and the gathering of the cones works in a similar way to the gathering of acorns. It is important for all seeds to move away from their place of origin, to get to new planting grounds, and the red squirrel accomplishes this. For the spruce, the squirrel may be even more important, for the spruce has a cone with so much resin that the seeds may not be released. The scales adhere to each other unless heat melts the resin or a squirrel takes the cone apart. The midden piles contain leftover seeds that might be gathered by mice and transported to different feeding sites where an overlooked seed might take root. If the area had a blowdown or a fire

while the seed germinated in the den, the tree might succeed and grow to maturity. Since the cones come every year and the tree produces thousands of seeds in its lifetime, it doesn't take a lot of planting for a tree to replace itself, but the system is one that involves a lot of variations.

The red squirrel doesn't build a big leafy nest like the grey. It uses cavities for a home and requires mature forests to survive. The red squirrel is an animal of the big trees and the virgin forest.

BEAVERS

An evening calm settled over the lake, the sky lost its rosy tints, and a purple greyness spread across the water. In the trees, a winter wren gave its long song, 101 notes strung together in a tinkling melody. A white-throated sparrow song burst out with startling clarity, and a Swainson's thrush gave a flute song of clear notes and echoing flourishes. There was little wind to disturb the pine trees. Water droplets from the paddles echoed and sounded foreign even though each paddler tried to make the strokes quiet and efficient. Then *bang*, a loud, sharp sound startled everything, leaving paddlers searching for breath that seemed to have escaped them.

A beaver had begun its nightly patrol and had been disturbed by a paddler, a loon, a feeding moose, or any number of possible occurrences that put the beaver territory out of order. With a loud bang of its tail, the beaver gave notice both to the intruder and to the beaver family.

The beavers rule the canoe country. I went through one series of lakes and streams where the lakes had disappeared and I had to substitute portages through sedges and shrubs because the beaver dams that had put the lakes in place had disappeared and they were not being replaced. All through the canoe country, the beaver sets water levels and regulates the water flow.

Their complex of dams, lodges, channels, and tree

cutting is well known and described so often that we lose our curiosity for the animal and stop looking closely, thinking we understand it so well. But beavers are much more than pond managers. They are also forest managers, helping to maintain edges for bird life and new succession for browsers.

Moose depend on beaver ponds and their abundant vegetation for their summer food. The large lakes are too deep to support such a concentration of aquatic foods. Wolves supplement their diet with beaver. Wood ducks nest in the natural cavities of trees that have drowned in the flowage, and all the active woodland animals use the stream water in the winter where the flow through the dams maintains open spots.

The beaver drew in the voyageur and the Indian. As a source of trade and discovery, the beaver was responsible for the development of the region.

Beaver (D. Cox)

(S. Kuchera)

MOOSE

BY MIKE LINK

A brown boulder breaks the flat plane of water as the canoe rounds the point and a new bay comes into view. It's a dark rock, shadowed and large. It barely catches your vision, except that as you scan the horizon, it seems to move. The water ripples, the rock grows, and suddenly a rack of antlers six feet across, a large muzzle dripping water and plants, and a pair of dark brown eyes emerge. The head shakes, the lips move, the plants disappear, and then the head plunges beneath the water again. You've just encountered a moose.

Each encounter with a twelve-hundred-pound moose is memorable. One fall, a student was walking a portage path and noticed some strange legs on the portagers coming from the other direction. He lifted his canoe to see who was in his way and saw a moose and its giant rack of antlers. The moose, on seeing a large, two-legged animal with a seventeen-foot rack of metal antlers, snorted.

That snort exacted an immediate flow of adrenaline in the student, who tossed the boat one way and ran the other. The sound of the boat landing on rock could be heard across the lake. With the trail now clear, the moose walked across to the other side.

The only time you need to fear a moose is in September, when the moose has only sex and fighting on its mind. Its neck is stiff and uncomfortable, and its rack is heavy. People have been treed for over a day by an irate bull. The bull moose loses the velvet on its antlers in August. At this time of year, the moose's diet is heavy in aquatic plants, but it also starts to graze in lowlands and sparsely stocked woodlands, where it eats a variety of shrubs.

Rutting and mating are usually in September, and the diet at this time is over seventy percent willow and aspen. The moose feeds in a wide variety of plant communities during the course of a year, which makes it more difficult to manage than the white-tailed deer. For adequate protection, the moose needs both large acreage and great diversity. The use of lowland fir and black spruce areas increases in October. The old adage about eating a balanced diet applies not only to humans. The moose adds mushrooms to its menu while moving into the fall woods. By mid-October, the mating and rutting are usually over.

In November, it is the lowland and upland open stands that are primary use areas. Statistics show that each month, the various plants browsed and the percent of the diet that they constitute changes. The aquatic diet that was so important in summer is absent for almost nine months of the year.

In the winter, the moose move from hardwood stands to dense conifer stands as the snow builds. A moose can move through snow that frustrates my snowshoes. It will explode in a cloud of white, leaving large holes where its body impacted. In two feet of snow, it moves as freely as it does in the summer. By December, it loses its antlers and begins to associate with other moose more than it did in summer. When the snow gets deep, moose will follow each other and use packed trails.

The spring bull has stubs of antlers covered by the fuzzy, blood-rich velvet common to all members of the deer family. The moose moves according to snow melt now, augmenting its winter woody diet with any newly exposed green growth.

The calves come in May and June, and they are expected to adapt to the adults' habits almost immediately. I watched a cow and calf cross a trail in front of me one June. The cow was intent on some distant destination and didn't even pause to look toward me. It just crossed the trail and plunged into the pond beside it.

The calf, long-legged and gangly, looked at me, hesitated, then hurried after its mother. She had begun to cross the lake by now, and the calf tried to walk on the soft bottom as rapidly as it could. I'm sure the smaller feet penetrated the muck more than the mother's large hooves.

The young one snorted some, but the cow seemed unconcerned and ignored each sound. Soon the cow was swimming, but the calf didn't seem to understand. I watched the nostrils on the small upturned snout bobbing in and out of the water as it continued to try walking. The snout would break the water, air would be expelled and quickly taken in, then down it went again.

The same routine lasted for the entire crossing. Going underwater isn't something alien to the moose. There are records of large bulls going completely under for food. Maybe this was part of the training.

In the spring, the moose will drink the rising sap on injured trees, eat fresh greens, linger at salt licks, eat lichens, and munch fresh leaves and twigs. In the summer, the ponds and lakes offer succulent new growth, as well as relief from mosquitoes. The moose's summer lifestyle means that each of us can hope that as we round the next point, we will be greeted with a big moose dripping water lilies from its snout.

A low, marshy area with stands of fir and spruce is the type of habitat wh

...se may be found in the fall. (D. Cox)

BEARS

BY MIKE LINK

Walking west from Whitefish Lake on an old remnant logging trail, I was intent on sounds. Jimmy and I were making our third breeding bird count — a June ritual that combines the masochistic feeding of thousands of blackflies, mosquitoes, and no-see-ums with the beauty of Swainson's thrush calls, the long songs of winter wrens, buzzy warblers, and other notes of spring.

With hearing sensitized to each note and the mind ready to analyze each sound, it is no trick to hear a bear rutting in the leaves. We heard it startled awake by our steps, listened to it stand up, move in the humus, and then stir the branches. Our noses soon confirmed the identification, and the forest suddenly became a different place.

I rushed into the woods to see the bear. In canoe country, we have only black bears, none of the more aggressive grizzlies, so danger is low. The black bear is many times stronger than I am and can rip me open with a stroke, but it is not an attacker.

Although black bears are much smaller than our mental image of bears, they have tremendous body strength, speed, and agility. This one was bothered by me, turned to look at my intrusion, then ambled off. Jim and I resumed our hike.

The trail we took at this point is short, and we were back on the forest service road in a few minutes. Our head nets still hung under the weight of flies looking for a meal, and we were sweaty from the long sleeves and pants that we wore for protection. The road let some breeze stir and sun penetrate.

Before long, our gait was easier and our nets were rolled back. We were enjoying the day, talking softly, and smiling at our experiences, when a black shape appeared ahead of us and disappeared over the next hill.

"Do you think that's our buddy from the trail?" Jim asked. We were a little more cautious as we walked, wanting to let the bear do whatever it wanted but still trying to satisfy our curiosity.

The bear went directly to our truck and began to nose around. This bear knew what trucks were and that treats might be found in them. We knew what he was up to now, so we approached more boldly to discourage any auto body repair work it might have in mind.

The bear moved, but not quickly. It went slowly into the woods and stopped. Jim and I got into the truck. The bear sat still and so did we. Its patience was not great, and soon it stood and began moving toward the van.

It was a deliberate movement — no hesitation, no veering, but slow and steady. The bear disappeared from view for a moment, then the ears appeared above the hood, followed by eyes and snout. I honked — one tap — before the feet and claws came up. The bear dropped and ran ten yards, took a few more steps, then stopped. It stood with its body parallel to the vehicle, looked at it, shifted its weight, and actually leaned against a small birch. The bear yawned. We laughed and drove on.

The bear is part of canoe country, but it is also a conundrum. Its wildness is not distinct and removed, like the wolves. It is strong and feared, cute and loved, a camp robber and pest.

On the Spider Lake end of the long Burntside portage, I encountered a bear that had learned that portagers would often bring over their food bag, set it down and return to the other end of the mile walk for more gear. By the time the portager returned, the bear would have substantially lightened the load.

On some heavily used routes, bears are often the official greeters. Nina-Moose Lake had a bear that appeared like magic when lunch was spread on a rock.

On the first canoe trip that I led in the BWCAW, we were camped near Basswood Falls and relaxing on the rocks. We had eaten our meal, washed the dishes, washed the grate and the rocks where food had spilled, and suspended our pack between two trees. We were enjoying the evening, when a panicked

Sloppy housekeeping habits by campers can cause the normally shy black bear to develop into a bothersome camp raider. (D. Cox)

camper came bursting through the woods.

"There's a bear in my camp."

"He'll leave. Don't worry about the black bear, he won't hurt you. Have you hung your food pack up?"

"Yes, my pack's hung, but my girlfriend's in the tent."

"Let's go check things out."

"Not me! I'm not going near that bear."

I walked over to the site. It was a mess. The girlfriend was in the tent, frightened and deserted. The bear was shuffling through the tidbits that it had spread out for easier picking, and it moved reluctantly when I shooed it into the woods.

The girl came out of the tent, relieved and mad. Her boyfriend was a new acquaintance. Both were from Chicago, and he had claimed to be an experienced woodsman. Next to their tent were all the plates and pots from dinner, unwashed. The groceries were hung in a cardboard box, so that the top was three feet off the ground and easy to reach into. The bear had no challenge here.

"I want to stay with your group," the girlfriend said.

"You'll be okay now. We really don't have room."

"I'm not staying with him."

We returned to my campsite. The bear was near us, and I tried to watch for it and listen. But by this time, the Chicago outdoorsman had my group riled up, and they were banging pans and plates in a makeshift German band, so that the bear and I could stumble into each other in total noise disorientation.

A second group that was visiting from another camp announced that they were staying with me, rather than going back to their camp.

I was starting to argue when I heard a scream and shout down at the lake. No time now. I canoed to this new site and found a father and son who had been visited by the burly camp inspector.

"He came right into the camp and grabbed our Duluth pack."

We talked. I checked for anything else that would attract the bear back. The camp was okay.

"Say Dad, maybe we should move down to his camp."

No thanks. As it was, I ended up with eight people in my four-man tent. It was a log jam in canvas.

Many people advocate not hanging packs. "Just keep them clean and absent of smells." Our Basswood Falls bear hit one more camp that night, grabbed a pack that contained both food and clothes, and ran off into the woods. The pack was not found again.

Some bears are so people trained that they have developed techniques that are both acrobatic and creative. On Alton Lake, good friends of mine who had canoed the area for over forty years had a bear shred their pack. It was hung between two trees, over eight feet above the ground. This was classic protection, but the bear knew the manual. It climbed to high branches and launched out into space to land on the pack and rip out its contents.

Not all bears invade tents and campsites, but they are smart animals. They are adaptable, with characteristics much like humans. Given the option, don't we go for convenience foods too? We have trained many bears by our slovenliness, by the spilled food, the fish guts we don't dispose of, the crumbs that are left out in hopes that the cute little animals will come out and be seen.

Bears are omnivorous. Like humans, they eat fish and fawns, blueberries and raspberries. They love sweet honey and tart ants. They require a lot of food to prepare for a winter denning. So the problem becomes a difficult one to solve—do you start with the person who leaves a mess or the bear who learns to enjoy it?

(P. and J. Sublett)

WOLVES

BY MIKE LINK

In the open, the snow was pounded to a crust by the wind. There were scallops, snowy barchan dunes, windrows, and ridges on the lake's surface. The forest was a gentler white, with mounds of snow perched on the branches and chest-deep drifts at the end of portage paths.

I skied alone, feeling the sting of the cold on my face as I crossed the open stretches and the warmth of sun in the protected. Skis vibrated on the hard pack, sunk in the drift, and glided over the protected woodland paths.

Solo skiing can be a mesmerizing experience — alone in white, green, and blue, at one with the easy motion of the skis and the feeling of muscles working in rhythm. The mind is caught in the cadence of the movement and drifts into the forest or the recesses of thought.

I was on a path that led from Sawbill to Smoke and Flame lakes. No one had put fresh tracks here for at least a week, and I relished the feeling of being alone. On a portage to Flame Lake, I was caught up in the patterns of snow on the branches, the intricate white and dark lines, when movement blurred across my peripheral vision.

A ball of fur, an explosion of white. Tremendous speed and energy. I stopped, my heart raced — a wolf! That had to be a wolf, the size, the color. I wanted to check its trail, so I floundered off the portage path into the deep soft snows that had been undisturbed all winter to find the deep body prints and indistinguishable tracks. I wanted perfect evidence, but I could only extract circumstantial.

The trail dipped down toward the lake and my skis had just begun to glide easily when my attention was refocused again. I dug in my poles and halted. In front of me was a large wolf, not more than 100 feet away. It paused, its fur soft and erect around the head. It stood its ground with no sign of fear or aggression.

A pup took off into the woods with the same abandon that the first had shown. The large wolf, a female, I guessed, stood and looked at me, turned toward the pups, turned toward a larger male that I had not seen, looked back at me, and seemed to weigh the alternatives before trotting off into the woods.

That left me and the large male to stare at one another. Eyes have magic. Aldo Leopold described the terrible loss of fire in the eyes of the last wolf he killed,

in an essay entitled, "Thinking Like a Mountain." It was a moment that turned his ecological philosophy around and shaped his future. Sigurd Olson, who did his thesis on timber wolves, described them as mysterious silhouettes. Now I had my own personal encounter, and as I stood there, I asked myself why the wolf didn't kill me. What reason was there for a hungry wolf to pass up 200 pounds of easy eating? I could have tried to stab him with my ski poles, cuffed him with my mittens, hurt his ears with my scream, but I could not have moved faster or farther than him. I could not have outfought him. I was at his mercy, and he did not take me.

We stood for a long time, and my mind raced with thoughts. The first time I heard a wolf call in canoe country, it was at such a distance that I had to strain to detect it, and my desire to have it be a wolf gave it more credibility than it should have had.

Later, I would have much stronger experiences, but the first distant wail would always be with me. Maybe it is the connotation of wildness that wolves represent that makes the vocalization so impressive. Maybe it is the sum effect of so many nursery fables that gives us a distorted feeling for the wolf.

People view wolves as slavering killers of domestic animals, the villains of cartoons and fairy tales, as evil incarnate, while simultaneously embracing dogs as domestic companions. It might be the sense of the unconquered that moves some of us but frustrates others.

There are those who want everything subservient to humankind and balk at the wildness of those creatures that will not be domesticated. We are still afraid of the dark, afraid of the sounds we hear but cannot explain, afraid of the silent stalkers.

To those who have listened with awe, who have felt the vibration of those voices, the wolf howl is a celebration of spirit and independence. It is a chorus of rebellion, a cry to be heard and to be left alone.

The wolf was wilderness, and it was right. Even if it had eaten me, it belonged. But the wolf did not eat me. It took a few steps toward me, stopped, stared, then loped in a grand arc away from me, out onto lake ice, and into the forest where the other three had gone.

There was no flicker of the tail, no parting howl, no gory trail of blood. It was an encounter between a part of the wilderness and one who sought wildness.

(R. Miles)

WHEN THE BUGS ARE DEAD

BY KATE CROWLEY

In the city, fall arrives on Labor Day. It doesn't matter if the thermometer rises to ninety degrees and everyone is wearing shorts and running their airconditioners full blast. In the mind of the urbanite, summer is gone and autumn has returned.

The kids head off to school once again, and the hardwoods that line the boulevards lose their summer green and fade into autumn, earthy shades. Soon the sidewalks will be covered by crunchy, crackly brown leaves that seem to be made especially for shuffling through. By Halloween, the season is well advanced and showing its age.

In the Boundary Waters, the arrival of fall is more subtle and can begin as early as mid-August. The sun is already drifting southward, the midday heat is not as intense as a few weeks before, and one is almost surprised by the early arrival of dusk. A few flowers continue to bloom, but the majority have spent their energy in the warmth of summer and now scatter their seeds to the wind and the soil below. Maples and aspen, though outnumbered by the more conservative, stately conifers, will brazenly begin to show a touch of red and yellow among their canopy of green.

For me, autumn is a favorite time to visit the Boundary Waters. I find nothing more uncomfortable than to be carrying a heavy pack, canoe paddles, and life preservers down a rocky portage trail on a hot day with the soggy, high humidity and a cloud of ravenous, winged blood suckers swarming over my sticky, sweaty, exposed skin. Sure, there is much to be said for the sunshine, warmth, birds, and flowers of the summer, but I prefer to go there when the bugs are dead and the people scarce.

It's not that I'm antisocial, it's just that I can better blend with the forests and lakes when there are fewer distractions. Fall in the canoe country is likely to have a preponderance of grey days, but this backdrop against the solid granite and steely blue waters adds to the atmosphere of retreat. The only sounds heard are the occasional warning cry of a blue jay or the distant croaking of a raven. The cheerful chirping of the warblers has faded with the flowers.

Now the sounds of paddle dipping into water and nylon jacket swishing with each stroke fill the void. The wind whispers through the pines, spreading rumors of the cold to come. With the increased precipitation in the autumn months, the forest floor erupts with a display almost as colorful as flowers. Walking down a slippery portage, with head bent to focus on each footstep, a flash of red or orange may catch the corner of your eye. Once you've discovered a mushroom near your feet, you stop and scan further and see that they're scattered all around, like jewels carelessly flung by a woodland fairy.

This is the season for fungi. The cooler temperatures and increased moisture are ideal conditions for their growth.

One of the more common kind of mushrooms seen pushing through the leaf litter are those of the genus *Lactarius*. These are known as milk mushrooms because of a milky fluid that flows from a broken stem. Their colors can range from pure white through shades of brown, yellow, orange, and red. These mushrooms start out with the common rounded cap, but as they age, the edges of the cap begin to bend upward, sometimes splitting in the process and exposing the rows of gills underneath. As this occurs, the center of the cap develops a dimple, which increases in size until it eventually forms a hollow cavity.

The most striking mushroom that you might see is as deadly as it is beautiful—the fly agaric, or *Amanita muscaria*. A flaming orange cap dotted with white or yellow "warts" perches on top of a white stalk. At the base of the stalk, you can sometimes see the egg-shaped volva from which the mushroom emerged. Look, but don't touch! Even on the darkest days, this mushroom seems to emit a warm glow.

Clustered together, close to the ground are the white puffballs and their close relatives, the brown earthstars. Both produce a "puff" of dark yellow

A pair of milk mushrooms show the characteristic cup shape of advanced age. (S. Kuchera)

spores when mature. The puffballs are one of the safest of the edible mushrooms, but as is true for any of the mushrooms, it is important to be sure of their identification before you eat them.

The earthstars look like little carved wooden flowers dropped on the ground. When they first emerge, they look like a brown puffball, but then the outer wall opens and curves back, splitting to form five "petals."

Mushrooms grow not only on the ground but on fallen logs and up the sides of tree trunks. One of the most unusual forms is the Tremellales, or jelly fungus. They are found on logs, stumps, or twigs and look like a convoluted mass of jelly. They may be flesh colored or brown. The yellow and orange species have been called witches' butter. In damp conditions, they look shiny and are slimy to the touch, but they shrivel up and turn hard in dry weather.

Another fungus found growing on dead stumps or logs is the coral fungus. These clusters of tightly packed branching stalks come in shades of pink, lavender, and orange, as well as chalk white, and look as though they've been picked up off the ocean floor and deposited in the forest. The branches may be soft and flexible or hard and rigid.

On the sides of trees are the polypores, or shelf mushrooms. These fungi attach themselves to the trunks and grow outward, forming rounded shelves. Some grow in clusters resembling composite flowers like the chrysanthemums. A popular name for one variety is turkey tail because of the concentric rings in shades of grey and brown, that emanate from the base. Others have glossy orange surfaces that look as though they've been shellacked. Another species is called the artist's conk because its pore surface has been used as a medium for etching pictures. On birch or aspen, you may find *Fomes fomentarius*, a smooth greyish cap with a strong resemblance to a horse's hoof (it is also called bell fungus).

The fungi play an important role in the forest ecology. Their vegetative parts (mycelium) are buried in the dead wood or leaf matter and very slowly break down the tough cellulose material so that it may be recycled and used by other organisms. Recently, it has been discovered that there are fungi that have a mutually beneficial relationship with living trees and shrubs (mycorrhizal associations). In this arrangement, the tree or shrub obtains nitrogen, phosphorous, and other nutrients that are normally difficult to come by, and the fungus obtains moisture and protection from the host plant. However, not all fungi are harmless or beneficial. There are parasitic fungi that will attack living plants and eventually cause their death. All of this living and dying is hidden from our eyes. What we see in the flashy, fantastic forms sprouting in the forest are the fruits of the fungi.

The mushrooms will wither with the coming cold. Autumn has a tentative grasp on this north country, and winter will inevitably arrive, sometimes earlier than we expect. A group of us were staying at the campground on Fenske Lake on the last day of September. Rain began in the evening, and we retired to our tents and fell asleep to the soothing sound of raindrops bouncing off the roof. Sometime during the night, the sound changed to a soft, wet plopping. Nearer morning, we heard strange cracking noises. When we unzipped the tent door, we discovered a world gone white. There was at least three inches of snow on the ground. The maples still held onto their scarlet leaves, even while their branches bent to the ground with the weight of the snow.

We left the Boundary Waters that day, and as we drove southward, the snow melted and faded from sight. Back in the canoe country the snow melted too—momentarily.

Overleaf (R. Miles)

WINTER WILDERNESS

BY MIKE LINK

The winter wilderness has a demanding beauty. The green trees are shrouded in white, branches droop with large snow snakes, bows bend with snow crowns, lakes lie still beneath many feet of snow and ice, and the ground is buried in whiteness. Air temperatures may plunge to forty degrees below zero, and breath freezes into stalactites on mustaches and hair.

It is a testing ground for preparation and skill, but it is also a realm of inspiration. The skier, snowshoer, and dog sledder have a wilderness that is more alone, more quiet, more remote than the canoeist can experience. Here only those who truly understand the wilds can venture. The temperatures and the conditions of winter need not be frightening, but they must not be underestimated.

The lakes still teem with life beneath their icy shrouds, but the life is different. The sunlight penetrates in diffuse rays, broken by the snow and ice roof. The plant life that can exist now is planktonic, not rooted. Food is reduced as a result, and animals have to adapt. The planktonic animals change. There are some that thrive in the winter lake, but others exist only as cysts on the lake floor.

Fish can roam the entire lake now. There is no temperature gradient as there was in the summer, and the lake turnover spread the oxygen from top to bottom. The pondweeds have died back for the winter, and the fish rely on dispersion for protection. Insect life is less abundant too, so the winter aquatic ecosystem is much more limited, just as is the terrestrial.

The streams serve the terrestrial animals' fresh water needs all winter, as the rapids keep an ice roof from completely enclosing the bed. Water levels change during the winter, so ice forms in layers with space in between, making the stream ice less structurally sound than the lake ice. Deer may take advantage of these thin sections and break open a drinking hole. Without this source of water, animals must convert snow or plant matter to water, and this makes a much greater demand on the animal's physiology. Otters slide down the banks of snow and into the open waters to dive and fish. Stone flies emerge in midwinter to mate and then return to the stream to lay eggs. Most fish spend their winters in the lake, but spawn up the streams near the end of the season.

On land, the plants seem to be helpless against the cold, and in some ways they are. Trees that lack a natural antifreeze don't live here. The conifers produce a form of alcohol that helps to protect them, while the deciduous trees use a natural sugar to reduce their freezing temperatures (we process this sugar from maples).

Some plants die off each winter to reproduce from seed again the next spring, but the boreal plants are mostly woody plants or ground plants that stay green all winter. These plants are ready for spring growth, maintaining their chlorophyl beneath the snow. In a land of short summers, this is important. For all the plants, snow is the key to survival. It protects the plants from frost, insulating them and holding the temperature near freezing. The pine seedlings require five years of snow insulation to develop their roots. After that period, they begin their upward growth.

The winter season is the great test; it is what distinguishes between native and visitor. Any migrant can survive blue waters and lush vegetation. Any tourist, whether bird or mammal, can handle the abundance of the summer. But to be a native requires an initiation from King Boreas. The winter is a time for the hardy.

The scarlet tanager might light up the dark woods, but it is the chickadee that scatters cheer below zero. This tiny bird ruffles its downy feathers and serenades the winter woods when competition has moved out and it has only a handful of species to share with.

Ravens soar beneath the ice crystal sun dogs and crash the silence with deep bass croaks. They wheel in the air with grace that is hidden in their rough black appearance.

Nuthatches and woodpeckers glean a harvest of

White-tailed deer (P. and J. Sublett)

Snowshoe hare (P. and J. Sublett)

overwintering insects from the bark of trees, crossbills disembowel the pinecones, and siskins, redpolls, and purple finch search for seeds scattered on the snows.

There are mammals that sleep out the winter, but the really tough ones find a way to make it on sparse food supplies. The moose and the deer browse on woody shoots that extend above the snow. Their legs sink in the snow, and they sleep curled up in depressions formed by their own bodies. The moose and deer have hollow hairs on their bodies, a natural insulation, and their legs function with lower temperature than the rest of the body. Like birds, the blood vessels of their legs pass close to one another to exchange heat and prevent venous blood that is too cold from shocking the heart.

On the snow, the tracks of winter tell the stories of the night's activities. There are signs of the winter-white snowshoe hare and weasel, one scraping the bark from a fallen aspen and the other hunting for any prey. There are deer mice tracks leading from their homes within snow-covered birds' nests and shrews that hope to catch and eat the mice.

Life is still "eat and be eaten" in the forest. Winter is a winding-down time, a time to set the equilibrium in balance. For the person who walks in the forest in this season, the woods have numerous stories to be read, and the lessons of the wildlife are applicable to the winter explorer.

Humans are vulnerable in the winter woods. Days are short and our mobility is limited by our aptitude for skis and snowshoes. We are testing out limits, relying on down, like the chickadee, or on trapped airspaces, like the deer. We must conserve our water or use more energy to convert snow to liquid, unless we cut through the ice or find an open stream.

If we learn these lessons, then the wind-packed lake is a fine surface to glide across and the soft forest snow is a pleasure to wander. This is the ultimate quiet, the final step in discovering the wilderness of canoe country.

Snow in the Boundary Waters can cover the ground from September to May. (D. Cox)

Sawbill Lake (D. Cox)

89

Listening Point (K. Crowley)

LISTENING POINT —A POSTSCRIPT

BY KATE CROWLEY

"Listening Point is a bare glaciated spit of rock in the Quetico-Superior Country. Each time I have gone there I have found something new which has opened up great realms of thought and interest. For me it has been a point of discovery and, like all such places of departure, has assumed meaning far beyond the ordinary."

Sigurd Olson

Growing up, I read about pilgrimages to holy places, but I never expected to make one myself. Then, in late September 1981, I found myself traveling north on a trip that came very close — a visit to a very special, spiritual place.

Through Northwoods Audubon Center, I had arranged a field trip to the Boundary Waters, with an emphasis on the writing and philosophy of Sigurd Olson. When we arrived in Ely, Mike decided to see if Sig and Elizabeth were home, and the news he came back with was even more exciting than we had anticipated. Not only could we spend the afternoon at Listening Point, but we were invited in to meet the Olsons.

We had not been prepared for such an invitation. Some of us had brought along Sigurd's books to read at camp, and we carried these inside with us. We sat in their den, on the sofa and on the floor, and watched Sig. He sat in a chair by a window, and though he would have been embarrassed and possibly annoyed at our awe, we felt we were in the presence of a legendary figure.

Here was a man who had fought some of the earliest environmental battles in the north country, before the environment became a popular cause. He was a man who had stood up for the natural world and faced derisive comments and physical challenges in order to preserve the Boundary Waters for generations to follow. This was the man who had written books that captured the beauty and satisfactions to be found in the woods of the North. For us, Sigurd Olson and the Boundary Waters were intertwined.

He was relaxed, gracious, and open, but we sat around the room in stunned silence. Sig had suffered a stroke and had some difficulty speaking, but we all sat intently focused on every word he said.

Although in his early 80s, Sig was still concerned about the struggles to preserve the wild places. He got up and went to a bookshelf, where he picked up a large three-ring binder filled with recent newspaper clippings and other published materials relating to environmental problems and government actions. It was at this time that James Watt was assaulting the environmentalists, and it was obvious that Sigurd was greatly distressed by the man and his power. He told us how important it was that we not give up the fight that will always face the natural and wild lands.

Those of us who had his books along asked him to sign them, which he did graciously. I had brought *Listening Point* with me, and it is even more special to me now, with Sigurd's inscription that says, "I hope some day you will find a Listening Point of your own."

We knew that our visit was tiring him, and so with many expressions of thanks to both him and Elizabeth, we left. Back in the van, we were silent at first, then like excited children, we all talked at once, of the man and his impact on us.

Mike drove us down a curving, hilly road until we came to the very unassuming turn-off to Listening Point. A small track — big enough for the van to squeeze through — led down to our parking spot. We carried our gear up a hill and some distance farther before we reached the point and the cabin. Visiting Listening Point was on the order of visiting Walden, but this was better, because the person who wrote about it was still alive, the cabin was still in use, and it was not open to the indifferent and the irreverent.

The cabin sat back from the water, but you could see the lake through the windows. The cabin looked as though it had grown up from the forest floor, with rough, weather-worn logs, windows on three sides of the building, and a massive stone fireplace filling the fourth wall. Inside were simple furnishings and a warm, lived-in feeling. The bunks were covered with bright red blankets, and the walls were decorated with books or special items, like a dream net—a symbolic, woven web that Sigurd described in *Runes of the North*. The table, benches, and countertops were worn smooth by years of human touch, and a few cooking utensils sat on the shelves near the "kitchen" window.

I wandered down the rocky spit until I came to what I thought must be the "bearberry ledge" that Sig described in *Listening Point*. The grey granite was almost hidden by deep carpets of greenish white reindeer lichen and other softer, dense, green mosses. The bearberry hugged the rocks and snaked in all directions. Mixed among these plants and standing at attention were the bright, red-capped, British soldier lichen. I sat down among the cushions of green and looked out over the dark water.

The sky was grey, and there was little wind to ripple the dark, cold lake. Near the water stood a gnarled old pine, like the one Sigurd saw silhouetted against the moon when he first spent a night camped on the ledge. As I sat and listened to all the deep quiet sounds of the point, I reflected on my life and love of the wilderness. I could feel that this was Sigurd's listening point and not mine, but I could understand why he found it so. *"There it was as I had dreamed, a composite picture of all the places in the north that I had known and loved."*

The pine on my left, the rocks and lake below, inspired me to try and capture their shapes for my memory. The act of drawing preserves the image better than any photograph I could take. It translates not only the scene but also my feelings onto a small piece of paper.

"I believe that what I have known there, is one of the oldest satisfactions of man, that when he gazed upon the earth and sky with wonder, when he sensed the first vague glimmerings of meaning in the universe, the world of knowledge and spirit was opened to him."

Later, we sat around the table and took turns reading favorite excerpts from Sig's books. I chose the first chapter from *Listening Point*, which describes the Olsons' quest for and discovery of that perfect place that would hold and add to their dreams and memories. The last paragraph of this chapter spoke to all of us and had special significance that late afternoon as we sat in the cabin with the shadows beginning to deepen. We could hear Sig's voice and picture him saying, *"I named this Listening Point because only when one comes to listen, only when one is aware and still, can things be seen and heard. Everyone has a listening point somewhere. It does not have to be in the north or close to the wilderness, but some place of quiet where the universe can be contemplated with awe."*

I decided to send the Olsons the drawing I had made while at the point, and a few weeks later, I received a note of thanks from Sig. Once again, he requested that I do what I could to protect and preserve the wilderness.

Years have passed, and yet the memory of that trip, the images, and the unexpected opportunities it provided are just as clear and colorful as if it happened yesterday. I often think how truly fortunate we were, because two months after our visit, Sigurd Olson was gone.

"The adventures that have been mine can be known by anyone."

Sigurd Olson

(M. Furtman)

PERSPECTIVES

BY MIKE LINK

The canoe country is a magnificent landscape that stretches along the Canadian border and north to the Arctic Ocean, but there is only one Boundary Waters Canoe Area Wilderness. It is a landscape covered by boreal forest and more than a thousand lakes, a landscape of Precambrian volcanics and Pleistocene glaciation. But it is more than all of that. It is a concept and a philosophy.

The BWCAW is a creation of law that embodies the belief of visionaries like Oberholtzer, Olson, Magie, Kelly, Hubachek, and Hinselman. It is an attempt to capture the virtues of wilderness in a place for people. It sets a limit to our recreation and forces us to slow down and to listen. It makes us less of a disturbance in the wild places and gives us more equal status with the wildlife.

In describing canoe country, we conjure up words like *solitude*, *quiet*, *timelessness*, and *beauty*, rather than *triumph* and *challenge*. The effort in getting there is not to reach a peak, a point of accomplishment, the effort is to reach a point where effort diminishes and we become one with our surroundings.

The concept of preserving this landscape is an idea that spans the sweep of our century and dates back to a time when wilderness was less rare and the movers were visionaries. The sanctuary was preserved through fights in Congress, in the courts, and in small town meetings. Solitude was the reward, but passiveness was not the way to achieve it.

Ernest Oberholtzer took on the money and the power of timber. Sigurd Olson stood up to criticism and verbal abuse in his home community. Bill Magie fought against flights into the area while his son ran a fly-in service. Hinselman was willing to sacrifice his job with the forest service. The warriors of the canoe country have fought with valor for ideals, and they have preserved a treasure.

The laws have been passed and the boundaries set, but the fights are not over. There are still battles over the enforcement of the laws. There are still tests of the resolve of the people who care. Mining, logging, recreation, and development are still threats to the future, but the threats reach far beyond the obvious. The air currents carry threats to the very existence of life in the form of acidic particles that settle like dust or fall in the rain and the snow.

This rugged land is a vulnerable land, with an Achilles heel that can be exposed by acid rain, runoff from logging, and leaching from mine tailings. The water is the lifeblood of the wilderness, and it cannot stand the impact of foreign bodies.

To protect this area means to watch over the earth, to keep the air clean, to reduce our demand on our natural resources. It means watching the forest plans, watching for development, and caring about wildness.

The Boundary Waters Canoe Area Wilderness cannot exist in a human-dominated world without humans who care. No wilderness can.

ABOUT THE AUTHORS

Mike Link has an enthusiasm for adventures—adventures as diverse as paddling a wild river, sailing the open seas, observing a wild bird, keying out a new flower, or reading a good book. Each experience is a challenge, and each new assignment is an opportunity. Mike has two children, Matt and Julie, who have shared outdoor experiences with their father.

As director of Northwoods Audubon Center, Mike also is an instructor in outdoor education for Northland College and the University of Minnesota at Duluth. His published works include *Journeys To Door County, The Black Hills/Badlands, Outdoor Education*, and *Grazing*, and numerous magazine and newspaper articles.

Kate Crowley's skills as a naturalist and writer were developed during her nine years at the Minnesota Zoo, where she supervised the monorail interpretive program and wrote articles for zoo publications. Her knowledge of wildlife and wilderness grew with participation in volunteer bird censusing for the Minnesota River Valley Wildlife Refuge and exploration of wild lands in the U.S. and abroad. She has served for five years on the board of the Minnesota Naturalist Association.

Kate is the proud mother of Alyssa and Jonathon. Her interests include almost any outdoor activity, especially sailing and bird-watching and more recently, exploring her new home in Willow River, Minnesota, with Mike.

Mike and Kate were married aboard the ketch *Izmir* and sailed Lake Superior on their honeymoon. They are coauthors of a new series for Voyageur Press covering wildlife and wild lands. *Love of Loons* and *Boundary Waters Canoe Area Wilderness* are the first two books in this series.

(M. Furtman)